BRITAIN'S FORGOTTEN FIGHTERS

OF THE FIRST WORLD WAR

BRITAIN'S FORGOTTEN FIGHTERS

OF THE FIRST WORLD WAR

PAUL R. HARE

FONTHILL

Fonthill Media Limited
Fonthill Media LLC
www.fonthillmedia.com
office@fonthillmedia.com

First published in the United Kingdom and
the United States of America 2014

ISBN 978-1-78155-197-4

Typeset in 10.5 pt on 13pt Sabon LT
Printed and bound by CPI Group (UK) Ltd, Croydon, CR0 4YY

Contents

INTRODUCTION 7

Chapter 1   ARMED SCOUTS 13
  Royal Aircraft Factory S.E.2 14
  Sopwith Tabloid 19
  Bristol Scout 27
  Martinsyde S1 38
  Royal Aircraft Factory S.E.4a 43
  Vickers ES1 48
  Royal Aircraft Factory B.E.12 53
  Martinsyde 'Elephant' 64

Chapter 2   PUSHERS AND PULPITS 75
  Vickers FB5 ('Gunbus') 76
  Airco DH1 88
  Royal Aircraft Factory B.E.9 93
  Airco DH2 99
  Royal Aircraft Factory F.E.8 111

Chapter 3   FLAWED FIGHTERS 123
  Vickers FB19 123
  Airco DH5 128
  Bristol M1 Monoplane 136
  Martinsyde F4 'Buzzard' 144

Chapter 4   THE FORGOTTEN FIGHTERS 151

ACKNOWLEDGEMENTS 159

Introduction

Almost everyone can name two British fighter aircraft from the First World War—the Royal Aircraft Factory S.E.5a and Sopwith Camel—designs which have often been called the Spitfire and Hurricane of that war. Aviation enthusiasts could probably go on to add the names of the Camel's predecessors such as the Sopwith Pup and Triplane, and its successors, the Snipe and Dolphin. They might also recite the French-designed Nieuport and SPAD, which also served with British forces; however, there were other fighters that saw action with the RFC, RNAS and RAF. Some were never intended to fight, but were hastily armed and pressed into service in a role their creators had failed to envisage. Some served in small numbers and away from the Western Front, but all made a vital contribution to winning the war. These forgotten aircraft and the brave young men that flew them in anger deserve to be remembered as are the famous aces in their well-known machines.

This is the story of those fighting aeroplanes whose names few people can recall, the now 'forgotten fighters' of the First World War. They fall into three distinct groups: those that were designed as high-performance, unarmed reconnaissance machines; fighters whose field of fire was considered more important than performance; and adequate fighting aircraft that lacked that certain something to make a great aerial opponent. For these forgotten fighters were all good aeroplanes, but were in some way flawed that prevented them being classed as great fighting aircraft.

The aeroplane was only adopted by the military a few years before the outbreak of the First World War in 1914, principally for reconnaissance. At the time, aerial fighting was an unknown quantity, although it was clearly being considered as *Flight* magazine explained in its 14 February 1914 edition:

There are two schools of thought regarding fighting in the air. The one holds that if an aeroplane is to fight, it must carry a passenger,

Never forgotten! The Sopwith Camel was the highest scoring British fighter of the First World War.

The Royal Aircraft Factory S.E.5a that was flown by Britain's highest scoring aces, including Mannock, Bishop and McCudden.

gun and ammunition. It will be so large and heavy that it will be slow, also it will lack any means of intercommunication necessary for combined action and it will be unable to come within range of a fast scout. The latter will come, get its information, and go, unmolested. It would appear that, for a time at all events, the fast scout will have the advantage. It depends largely on the number of fighting machines available. The other view is that fighting in the air must occur if results are to be obtained. Given that one side has sufficient fighting machines, it should be impossible for an unarmed scout to approach the point where it desires to glean information.

The RFC appears to have embraced both views and added to its growing fleet of general purpose aeroplanes a number of fast scouting machines. It was therefore hoped that these aircraft could evade enemy scouts as well as gather information vital to British operations. Also, it was anticipated that the armed aeroplanes would be able to protect unarmed machines as they went about their business.

Royal Navy pilots shared the view that armed aeroplanes were essential, Lt Clark-Hall writing in early 1914:

Typical of the RFC's vulnerable two-seat general purpose aeroplanes was the Royal Aircraft Factory's B.E.2c that was built in large numbers by various contractors before the need to adequately arm such machines became apparent.

Machine-gun aeroplanes are (or will be) required to drive off enemy machines approaching our ports with the intention of obtaining information, or attacking with bombs, our magazines, oil tanks or dock yards... I would strongly advocate having, by the end of 1914, at each of our home ports and important bases at least two aeroplanes mounting machine guns for the sole purpose of beating off or destroying attacking enemy machines.

With the introduction of the Fokker monoplane fighter in the summer of 1915, the Germans gained ascendancy in the air. This was not due to the type possessing a significant advance in design or performance, but simply because it was effectively armed with a forward-firing machine gun mounted in front of the pilot and synchronised to fire past the blades of the spinning propeller. By the end of 1915, these had been grouped to form fighter units to attack Allied aeroplanes. So bad did the situation become that in January 1916, the RFC issued a general order stating that:

The Fokker Eindecker whose forward-firing machine gun created havoc when it was introduced on the Western Front in the summer of 1915.

...until the Royal Flying Corps are in possession of a machine as good as, or better than, the German Fokker ... It must be laid down as a hard and fast rule that a machine proceeding on reconnaissance must be escorted by at least three other fighting machines.

At first, one or two armed aeroplanes were issued to RFC squadrons for escort duties. However, it was not until March 1916 that it was decided that these should be grouped together in specialist squadrons. This move, together with the introduction of newer designs, allowed the RFC to regain some measure of control in the skies over the Western Front and allow reconnaissance and bombing machines to carry out their duties without undue risk of attack. The fighters would patrol behind enemy lines, beyond the area in which the slower machines were working, and drive off enemy aircraft before they could shoot them down. At the same time, they would prevent enemy aircraft crossing the lines to carry out their own missions. Air fighting was carried out only to render the work of Army co-operation and reconnaissance machines possible while attempting to prevent similar activities by the enemy.

CHAPTER 1

Armed Scouts

Towards the end of 1911, even before the RFC came into existence, a competition was announced in Parliament to be held the following August in order to determine the most suitable aeroplane with which to equip the Army's air service. Marks would be given for high speed; for the ease with which entrants could be erected and dismantled so that they could accompany an army on the march; ability to land on a rough surface; and for the view from the cockpit. A host of other features, all considered desirable in a military aeroplane, were specified for the guidance of entrants, but there was not even the slightest suggestion that potential military aeroplanes should be armed. Their future role was seen as that of reconnaissance and it was thought that speed would provide protection from enemy aircraft. For example, on 15 May 1913, Major F. H. Sykes, then officer commanding the RFC (Military Wing), expressed his opinion in a letter to the War Office about the Corp's requirement for a reconnaissance machine that:

> One of the most important lines of development which should in my opinion be pursued is towards machines of large radius of action for strategically reconnaissance. Such machines should, in order to enable them to evade hostile aircraft, be possessed of the highest practicable speed.

At the outbreak of war, the role of aeroplanes remained that of reconnaissance, scouting further ahead and faster than the cavalry could go. Fast aeroplanes therefore became known as scouts, a name that was applied to all single-seat machines throughout the war. When the need for fighter aircraft emerged for defence against enemy fighters, a number of fast scouting machines were armed as a stopgap measure until better designs became available. Although they brought down few enemy aircraft, they proved a worthwhile deterrent to any greater level of aggression by their opponents. Also, that they met with any success in a role for which they had never been intended or designed is proof of their excellent qualities as flying machines.

In approximate chronological order these armed scouts were as follows:

ROYAL AIRCRAFT FACTORY S.E.2

The Royal Aircraft Factory at Farnborough—a Government-run establishment that was first organised in 1878 to construct observation balloons for the Army—designed what was probably the world's first high-speed scouting aeroplane towards the end of 1912 as its superintendent, Mervyn O. Gorman, considered that speed would be an unarmed reconnaissance machine's best defence. The new design was originally designated Blériot Scout No. 1, or B.S.1, to signify that like the famous cross-Channel machine, it was a tractor design. However, before it was completed, its designation was changed to S.E.2 ('Scouting Experimental No. 2'), the Factory having revised its system of nomenclature.

Design work was carried out by Geoffrey de Havilland who was then employed at the Factory as both test pilot and designer, and included every possible innovation to ensure lightness, streamlining and speed. Power was provided by a 100-hp Gnome rotary engine although the engine mountings and cowling were sufficiently large to accommodate an engine of 140 hp should one be made available. The forward fuselage, to which the wings and undercarriage were attached, was built around a four longeron box girder faired to a round cross-section to match the engine cowling, the tail section being a moulded plywood monocoque. The biplane wings were separated by one pair of interplane struts at each side and cross braced in a single bay, the first time such a simple bracing system had been employed. The spade-shaped tailplane was fitted with a one-piece elevator, the low-aspect-ratio-balanced rudder mounted on top of the fuselage. The rather sturdy looking twin-skid undercarriage was supported on four struts and the wheel discs were covered in fabric to reduce resistance.

De Havilland made the first flight in the S.E.2 on 13 March 1913 and reported favourably on its performance and handling, although he realised that the rudder was too small, especially as the covered wheels added keel area forward. Consequently, de Havilland designed a larger one, but continued to fly the machine as built while waiting for the new surface to be fabricated. Climb was recorded at 800 feet per minute,

The B.S.1/S.E.2 as it first appeared with the buildings of the Royal Aircraft Factory in the background. The presence of onlookers was usual as the airfield was a public common.

the maximum speed averaging the results of a number of runs over a measured course at 91.7 mph. However, this performance had not been achieved without some sacrifice and the minimum speed was about 50 mph, a very high figure for those days.

On 27 March, de Havilland was flying the S.E.2 over Farnborough Common and made a turn at a height of about 100 feet when a sideslip developed. With the inadequate rudder, de Havilland was unable to control the machine and it entered a flat spin and crashed. De Havilland's injuries included two badly sprained ankles, a broken jaw and the loss of some teeth. Damage to the machine was more extensive with the cost of repair being estimated at £900. While seeking authorisation for the work, O'Gorman also requested an additional £425 to purchase an 80-hp Gnome engine, claiming that with 100 hp, the machine was too fast for the average pilot. A surprising admission about an aeroplane specifically built for high speed, but O' Gorman was merely sowing seeds for his future plans to build an even faster design.

With de Havilland in hospital, the redesign of the S.E.2 was undertaken by Henry Folland and included a new streamlined engine cowling and tail surfaces with a semi-circular tailplane. Also fitted were dorsal and ventral fins, each triangular in shape, and a high-aspect-ratio rudder, the bottom edge of which was shod in steel for use as a landing skid, the rudder post being sprung to absorb shocks.

It was 12 October before the repaired machine is recorded as having flown again with de Havilland at the controls. Although slower, it was found to climb almost as well as previously, the reduction in weight more

The S.E.2 after modification by Henry Folland photographed on the edge of Farnborough Common from which test flying took place.

or less compensating for the lower power. On 5 November, O'Gorman informed the Assistant Director of Military Aeronautics that although the S.E.2 was complete and testing had finished, he wished to retain it for use in trials connected with the true high-speed aeroplane he planned to build next. This was not to be, although the War Office appears to have taken some time to reach its decision and on 23 December, O'Gorman was instructed that the S.E.2 was to be handed over to the RFC for service use. Despite O'Gorman's unheeded protests that the machine was experimental, the S.E.2 joined No. 5 Squadron based at Farnborough in January 1914. It was flown by at least four pilots who confirmed that the machine was easy to fly and land, although its shallow gliding angle meant that it would be hard to land in a field surrounded by trees. The view of the ground was considered good—a useful attribute in a reconnaissance aeroplane—but there was no forward view when climbing or taxiing on the ground. It was generally thought to be very fast, which it undoubtedly was, by standards of the day.

After just two months in service, the S.E.2 was returned to the Factory for an overhaul costing £465. The monocoque rear fuselage was replaced with a conventional fabric-covered structure formed around four longerons and faired to a circular cross-section similar to the forward fuselage. New horizontal and vertical tail surfaces were fitted with the fins and rudder increased in area, a separate tail skid provided, and the undercarriage was replaced with new components of a similar design to the original. A spinner was fitted to the propeller hub and cable bracing replaced with swaged streamlined wires, a new innovation called, at least by the Royal Aircraft Factory, as Rafwires. It was now officially designated as the 'S.E.2 Rebuilt' and was given the service serial number 609. It was test flown on 3 October 1914 by

The S.E.2 after rebuilding with modified vertical tail surfaces and a new and more conventional rear fuselage.

Another view of the rebuilt S.E.2 showing its very clean lines to advantage.

Frank Goodden who had replaced de Havilland as the Factory's chief test pilot. Sadly, a skid broke on landing, delaying the completion of its testing and was not returned to the RFC until 20 October.

By 27 October, it had joined No. 3 Squadron in France as a fast scout. Initially, its only armament was a service revolver carried by the pilot. However, when it began escort duties, it was armed with two Lee-Enfield service rifles, their shoulder stocks cut off, fixed to the fuselage sides and aimed outwards at an angle to fire clear of the propeller. Firing such weapons (which were bolt action with a conventional trigger) with gloved hands in an icy slipstream must have proved very difficult and aiming could only have been a matter of luck, so it is of little surprise that no combat victories were achieved.

In March 1915, it was considered to be unfit for further active service and was returned to the Aircraft Park, and from there was sent back to England. Although as the first true scout, there was some talk of it being considered for preservation, but this did not happen and it was struck off RFC charge, its eventual fate being unrecorded.

The S.E.2 in RFC service. It appears to have a roundel painted on the rudder rather than the Union Jack that was common in the early days of the war.

SOPWITH TABLOID

Towards the end of 1913, a trim little biplane emerged from the Sopwith factory at Kingston-upon-Thames. The Sopwith Tabloid may have been inspired by the S.E.2, although credit for its initial concept is generally given to Sopwith's Australian protégé, Harry Hawker, with detailed design being carried out by Thomas Sopwith and Fred Sigrist. Construction was entirely conventional with a wire-braced box girder fuselage and single-bay wings, but showed the delicacy common in Sopwith-built machines. Designed for high speed, either for sport or scouting, it had two seats, side by side, with the pilot on the left and was powered by an 80-hp Gnome rotary engine fitted into a bull-nosed cowling enclosing its forward engine mounting (an unusual but practical feature). Lateral control was by warp and the balanced rudder had no fin. As was usual for the period, a twin-skid undercarriage was fitted, the axle bound in place with rubber shock cord. It was assembled and tested at Brooklands as was normal Sopwith practice, and then on 29 November 1913, was formally tested at Farnborough where, loaded with a pilot, passenger and fuel for a 2½ hours flight, it achieved a top speed of 92 mph. Its initial climb was at the rate of 1,200 feet per minute and its lowest speed just 37 mph, giving a remarkable speed range. Once tests were completed, Hawker flew the Tabloid to Hendon, impressing the large crowd in attendance at the Saturday air show with two very fast circuits before landing.

It would appear that the machine was initially referred to at Sopwith as the StB or 'Stunt Bus', but acquired the nickname 'Tabloid' due to its compact size and cramped cockpit. At the time, this was a trademark belonging to the drug company Burroughs, Wellcome & Co. whose very public objection to its use in connection with the new aeroplane was sufficient to ensure that the name stuck.

Within two weeks of its public debut, the prototype Tabloid had been crated and shipped to Australia, accompanied by Harry Hawker for demonstration in the hope of attracting sales in Hawker's homeland. Sailing on RMS *Maloja*, they reached Adelaide on 19 January 1914 and made over sixty flights, some with civic dignitaries and government officials including the Minister of Defence as passengers.

Authorities in the UK were clearly as impressed with its performance as the crowds at Hendon had been and on 18 December 1913, placed an order for nine examples at a cost of £1,075 each as fast scouts. Three more aircraft were added to the order early in the following year. These aircraft differed from the prototype in having a fixed triangular fin with a plain rudder and a single seat placed on the fuselage centreline,

The newly completed Tabloid at Brooklands with the banked motor racing track in the background.

Hawker taking off from Brooklands in the prototype Tabloid.

making the cockpit comparatively roomy. The mountings were modified, making the nose more pointed, and the undercarriage struts were raked forwards. Also, the skids were slightly longer with a split axle, giving each wheel independent movement that would become typical of Sopwith.

Aircraft produced after June were fitted with ailerons for lateral control and had a simple vee undercarriage, retaining the split axle arrangement. As was usual for the period, its instrument panel was simple and included only an altimeter, air speed indicator, compass, tachometer, fuel gauge and air-pressure gauge together with a hand-air pump, fuel tank selector and ignition switches.

The first production example was test flown at Brooklands on 11 April 1914 by Howard Pixton who had taken over Hawker's duties while he was in Australia. The following day, it was flown by Harold Barnwell (Vickers' test pilot and flying instructor in the company school) who performed the first ever loop carried out by a Brooklands pilot, although his first attempt was not entirely satisfactory. After landing, Barnwell discussed what he had done to complete the manoeuvre with Thomas Sopwith, then took off again and looped the little scout a further three times with great success. Thereafter, Pixton flew the machine to Hendon, although the reason for the journey is unrecorded.

Meanwhile, what was almost certainly one of the production machines intended for the RFC, was fitted with floats and a 100-hp engine for entry into that year's Schneider Trophy race. It was taken to Hamble for testing but proved to be unstable, turning nose over and sinking. Recovered a few hours later at low tide, it was returned to the works and dried out, the initial single float modified by sawing it in two. Although the engine showed some corrosion as evidence of its immersion, it still ran. It was therefore overhauled and retained with Sopwith engaging engine expert Victor Mahl to get the best possible performance from it.

There being no time for a return trip to Hamble, the Tabloid was tested without prior permission on the River Thames near to the Sopwith works on 7 April, but the Thames Conservatory Board objected and it had to be removed from the water. Tests resumed the next day further downstream close to Richmond on the tidal section of the river controlled by the Port of London Authority. Its attitude, when on the water, was incorrect with the rear of the floats submerged and their noses clear of the water. Also, the elevators, if lowered, touched the water. However, the Tabloid floated safely, if rather inelegantly, and made a successful take off with no time for further amendments.

Engine expert Victor Mahl, Howard Pixton and Thomas Sopwith in front of the Sopwith entry to the 1914 Schneider Trophy.

Pixton leaning against the wing of the trophy-winning Tabloid at Monaco. The mechanic crouching on the float may have been attempting, without conspicuous success, to adjust the balance as the rear of the floats and trailing edges of the elevators are under water.

With 'SOPWITH' painted along each side of the fuselage in the largest letters possible and the racing number '3' on the rudder, it was taken to Monaco where on 20 April and piloted by Pixton, it won the race. This was staged as a time trail with each machine completing the course individually at an average speed of 87 mph. This was followed by a further two laps at 92 mph to create a new world speed record for seaplanes. When offered a glass of champagne to toast his victory, Pixton responded 'Mine's a small Bass.'

Deliveries to the RFC continued, although one machine, 378, turned over on landing at Farnborough on 22 April. Considered beyond repair, it was later tested to destruction by the Royal Aircraft Factory in order to verify the strength of its construction.

Hawker—who had returned from Australia on 6 June with the prototype Tabloid—delivered the last of the batch of twelve to Farnborough on 4 August 1914. The much travelled prototype, now fitted with a vee undercarriage and with the fabric removed from its rear fuselage supposedly as an aid to aerobatics, was impressed into RFC service with the serial 604 (Sopwith was paid £900). Although the type was already in service with some RFC squadrons—for example, 381 having been with No. 3 Squadron since 1 July—none went to France when the RFC flew out on 13 August. However, four examples were shipped out in crates with the Aircraft Park on 18 August, the only spare aeroplanes available at the time. Two of these were issued to No. 3 Squadron on 24 August, but both were wrecked by the middle of September. James McCudden, then an air mechanic with No. 3 Squadron, later recalled:

> Soon after landing, we saw two very fast machines come in and on inspection they proved to be Sopwith Tabloids flown by Norman Spratt and Gordon Bell. These machines were very speedy for those days, doing nearly 90 mph, as well as having a good climb. They did not avail us much as fighting machines in that they were not fitted in any way with firearms, but they could, and did, perform excellently from the scouting point of view.

On 28 August, Second Lt Norman Spratt, a former test pilot serving with the RFC Reserve, achieved one of the first aerial victories of the war. At about 5.30 p.m., an Albatros C1 two-seater dropped three bombs onto the temporary airfield on the racecourse at Compiègne. This attack did little damage although one bomb landed close to the latrines, panicking an NCO who was using the facilities at the time. Spratt took off and gave chase, and although his Tabloid was unarmed, forced the enemy

Tabloid, 326, that served at the Central Flying School in 1915.

to land by flying aggressively as if to attack. Three days later and armed with a revolver, Spratt attacked another enemy aircraft and fired thirty rounds at it, but without visible result.

386 remained with the Aircraft Park until 26 December when it was issued to No. 4 Squadron, but was struck off charge after a few weeks. The last remaining machine was returned to England on 4 February 1915, thus ending the RFC's operational employment of the Sopwith Tabloid, although a few carried on serving with training units for a short period (326 saw service at the Central Flying School during 1915).

The little Sopwith was also ordered prior to the war by the Admiralty for use by the RNAS, although the Navy refused to recognise the name Tabloid and referred to the type as the Sopwith Scout. The RNAS seems to have been better pleased with the type than the RFC and so during September 1914, the Admiralty purchased three unwanted examples from the War Office, paying the full price of £1,075 for 394 and 395, but only £800 for 604. The machines were renumbered with serials from a batch allocated to the Navy with 167–169, the latter serial being assigned to 604. These machines joined a unit based at Antwerp under the command of C. R. Samson towards the end of September 1914, although 169 crashed a few days later.

On 8 October, the remaining two airworthy machines piloted by Sqn Cdr Spenser Grey and Ft Lt R. G. Marix set off to bomb the airship sheds at Cologne and Düsseldorf. Grey's efforts were frustrated by poor visibility and he bombed the railway station at Cologne instead. However,

Tabloids under production at Sopwith's works at Kingston-on-Thames during 1914.

Marix in 168 dropped his bombs on the airship shed at Düsseldorf from just 600 feet, setting fire to the Zeppelin inside, destroying it completely. Both machines returned to Antwerp but had to be abandoned when the airfield was evacuated due to an enemy advance on 14 October 1914.

No. 1 Squadron RNAS was assigned four Tabloids on 1 December 1914, but they achieved nothing of note. Samson's unit had at least one on strength during the early part of 1915 and was armed with a Lewis machine gun above the centre section on a mounting devised by W/O J. G. Browridge and Lt T. Warner, but there is no record of its use. Although only thirty-six Tabloids were built, the type's career did not end there for the float-mounted version that won the Schneider Trophy was adopted in November 1914 as a seaplane by the RNAS. Its float arrangement was modified slightly to improve its balance on the water and it was christened the Sopwith Schneider.

At least 136 Schneiders were built by Sopwith, later examples having an enlarged fin with a curved leading edge and served throughout the war. Although too frail to operate directly from the sea unless unusually calm, efforts to employ it to intercept Zeppelins proved to be less than satisfactory; however, the Schneider was ideal when operated from seaplane carrier ships. On 8 August 1915, one example piloted by Ft Lt W. L. Welsh made the first take off from the *Campania*, a converted Cunard liner. Mounted on a wheeled dolly and with the ship steaming at 17 knots into a 13-knot wind, the Schneider was airborne in an astonishing 130 feet. The Schneider left the deck with twenty feet spare

Sopwith Schneider, 3804, with a launching dolly under the floats and the tail on a trestle.

Unidentified Sopwith Baby showing the horseshoe-shaped cowling that enclosed its more powerful engine and distinguished the type from its predecessors.

and landed on the water where it was hoisted back on the ship. Indeed, the deck proved too short for use by any other type of aircraft and after three successful take offs, was returned to the shipyard for modification.

However, the Schneider served throughout the war in the Mediterranean, Aegean and Red Seas. From the Schneider was developed the Sopwith Baby that was basically the same aeroplane, but fitted with a Clerget engine of 110 or 130 hp in a horseshoe-shaped cowling. Sopwith built 100 examples with further aircraft contracted at Blackburn and Fairey. Attempts to fit a synchronised machine gun proved unsuccessful and although some were armed with a Lewis gun firing clear of the propeller, the type never engaged in combat, but carried out anti-submarine patrols and scouting missions.

BRISTOL SCOUT

Frank Barnwell—who in 1909 made the first powered flight in Scotland in an aeroplane he and his brother, Howard, built—joined the British and Colonial Aeroplane Company Ltd of Bristol as a designer. Barnwell went on to design the famous Bristol Fighter, Bulldog and Blenheim before he was tragically killed in a flying accident in 1938. At the suggestion of the Bristol Aeroplane Company's test pilot, Harry Busteed, Barnwell designed a neat little single-seat biplane that he drew in a simple notebook, sending carbon copies to workshops from which to manufacture the components. Completed in early 1914, it had a wingspan of just 22 feet with one pair of interplane struts each side and the usual wire-braced box girder fuselage with the forward portion of the four longerons being of ash and the after part spruce. The fuselage was clad in aluminium, aft of the engine cowling and almost as far back as the cockpit, the remainder being fabric. The tailplane which, like the wings had outwards raked tips, was set at a negative angle of incidence to give stability and the rudder had a small balance area ahead of the rudder post. A wooden vee undercarriage was fitted and the wheels were uncovered. Power came from an 80-hp Gnome rotary engine that had been previously fitted to a Coanda monoplane and had been recovered and refurbished after crash landing on water. This was enclosed in a horseshoe-shaped cowling, open at the bottom, and drove a two-blade propeller. It was taken by road to Larkhill, home of the company's flying school, where it was test flown by Busteed on 23 February 1914, achieving an impressive 95 mph.

Following testing the new machine now named the Scout, it was put on display at the fifth annual Aero Show where it was much admired.

The first Bristol Scout jacked up into flying position and showing its very trim lines.

The Scout after modification with the racing number '1' on the rudder.

When the show closed, the Scout did a great deal of flying in the hands of Harry Busteed who at Easter flew it from Larkhill to Brooklands in just 27 minutes—although with the aid of a following wind. It was then returned to the company's works at Filton to be fitted with new wings, their span increased by 31 inches in order to improve the rate of climb, together with other modifications, which included enclosing the engine within a full circular cowling. Following these modifications, it was flown to Farnborough for demonstration to the RFC and its top speed, when measured on 14 May, had increased to over 97 mph. At least one pilot reported a swing to the left on take-off, but this was easily controlled by the application of right rudder as soon as it started and was something that most pilots would handle instinctively.

It was then sold without its engine for £400 to Lord Carbery, a keen sporting pilot, who fitted it with the 80-hp Le Rhône engine that had previously powered a Morane-Saulnier monoplane. Following a forced landing at Castle Bromwich during a race from Hendon to Manchester and back, the Scout was fitted with a new undercarriage and wider track. Carbery then competed in the London-Paris-London race, making the outward flight non-stop in 3 hours and 56 minutes. In the haste of preparing for the return journey, only one of two petrol tanks was refilled and starved of fuel, the engine stopped over the Channel, obliging Carbery to come down in the water. The Scout stayed afloat long enough for the pilot to be rescued by a passing steamer, but the machine could not be hoisted aboard and only the forward fuselage and engine were saved.

Meanwhile, two further examples had been built to a War Office order differing from the original in that all flying wires were duplicated, the undercarriage had the wider track of Carbery's machine in its final form, and the engine cowlings were stiffened with external ribs. These machines were numbered 633 and 648, and were assigned to Nos 3 and 5 Squadrons, RFC, both going to France in September 1914. The No. 3 Squadron machine was usually flown by Lt R. Cholmondley and was later armed with two cut-down service rifles fixed to the fuselage sides and angled to fire clear of the propeller. No. 5 Squadron's example was armed with a service rifle with the shoulder stock removed on the starboard side, its pilot, the squadron's commanding officer, Major J. F. A. Higgins, also usually carried a pistol and grenades. Higgins, who wore a monocle to correct the sight of one eye, loved flying the nimble Scout, but failed to hit anything he shot at and was wounded in the thigh by a bullet from an intended victim. No. 5 Squadron returned 648 to the depot, presumably for repair, in November 1914 where it remained until the following March when it was reissued to No. 4

Squadron. Impressed with its performance, the War Office placed an order for a further twelve Scouts (serials 1602–1613) on 5 November 1914, the Admiralty also placing an order for use by the RNAS two days later. Curiously, Bristol delivered one of the Navy's batch, 1243, first and then between 23 April and 13 June 1915, completed the War Office order before continuing with deliveries to the Navy. By September, Nos 1, 2, 3, 4, 5, 6, 7, 10, 12 and 16 Squadrons, RFC, each had a single Scout on strength while No. 8 Squadron had two. A No. 12 Squadron pilot recalled that:

> The Bristol was a delightful little machine with an 80-hp Le Rhône engine. One was allocated to each of the B.E. squadrons and was the cause of infinite jealousy among pilots as it usually became the perquisite of the senior flight commander.

Further orders were placed while the first batches were still being built with the War Office ordering seventy-five examples (4662–4693 and 5291–5327) in March 1915 and the Admiralty ordering fifty (3013–3062). These production machines were designated Scout C with British and Colonial considering retrospectively, the prototype to have been Type 'A' and the two subsequent examples Type 'B'. They had a modified engine cowling and a revised forward fuselage decking with a slight change of shape to the cockpit cut-out. Although the 80-hp Gnome remained the usual engine, delivery problems meant that some aircraft were completed with a Le Rhône of similar power. The change necessitated some modifications to the oil system as it was found that the Le Rhône engine was starved of oil while taxiing. The Navy insisted that all its machines should have the Gnome engine, which was generally considered more reliable, an important consideration when flying over water. However, deliveries were slow and the last of their batch of fifty was not delivered until 25 March 1916.

Captain Lanoe George Hawker of No. 6 Squadron, together with his mechanic, Earnest Elton, devised a mounting for a Lewis machine gun on the portside of his Bristol Scout, 1611, angled outwards to fire clear of the propeller and on 25 July 1915, Hawker, flying alone, attacked three enemy aircraft in succession. The first managed to escape but the second was believed to be damaged and the third crashed over British lines, its crew being killed. Hawker was awarded the Victoria Cross for his gallantry in tackling what were considered to be superior forces, each of the enemy machines having a dedicated gunner with a pivoting machine gun, while his own field of fire was limited.

Bristol Scout, 1611, with the obliquely-mounted Lewis gun devised by L. G. Hawker.

Hawker achieved further victories in the Scout and on 7 September, engaged an enemy scout and closed to 50 yards before opening fire with the enemy falling away in a dive, its fatal descent witnessed by artillery batteries. Despite Hawker's success, his angled gun was not widely adopted as it was difficult to aim accurately and the Scout was armed with a Lewis gun mounted on top of the centre section where it could be aimed straight ahead. However, changing ammunition drums, which at that time held just forty-seven rounds, was more difficult. At least one RNAS machine had its gun fitted immediately ahead of the pilot where aiming and changing drums were simpler, the occasional bullet through the machine's own propeller being accepted. Single holes were plugged and bound with tape, the propeller being scrapped after the third hole.

During March 1916, a Scout was tested with an early form of the Vickers-Challenger mechanical interrupter gear with a belt-fed Vickers machine gun mounted ahead of the pilot; however, although a few machines saw service thus armed, such an installation was not widely adopted perhaps due to the additional weight. The RNAS also armed a few of its Scouts with the Vickers gun, but these were fitted with the Scarff-Dubrovsky interrupter gear that the Navy preferred.

Deliveries of the final variant, the Scout D, began in February 1916, further orders having been placed both by the War Office and the Admiralty. This incorporated some further refinements, including a further enlarged rudder and streamlined bracing wires. Later examples had smaller ailerons and, as in response to feedback from squadrons

Captain Lanoe Hawker was awarded the Victoria Cross for his courage in attacking a well-armed foe in his Bristol Scout.

operating the type, had their wing-tip skids moved from under the interplane struts to a position closer to the wing tip. Some, especially the Navy's batches 8951–9000 and N5390–5400, were fitted with the 100-hp Monosoupape engine, its larger diameter necessitating a modified cowling. At least three examples, 5554–5556, were powered by the 110-hp Clerget engine in a further modified cowling, necessitating a step in the fuselage sides with 5555 also having a large diameter shallow spinner fitted to its propeller boss, anticipating the arrangement later fitted to the Bristol M1 monoplane.

A total of 374 Scouts were built by the British & Colonial Aeroplane Company and comprised the original prototype, later designated Type 'A', the two Type 'B' machines, 161 Type 'C' and 210 Type 'D'. At least three more, B740, B763 and B793, were created from spares and parts recovered from damaged aircraft by the Southern Aeroplane Repair Depot based at Farnborough.

The Scouts were used both as escorts and interceptors, being hastily dispatched when enemy aeroplanes were spotted. Encounters with the enemy became more frequent, but were often inconclusive. For example,

A Scout with the rather clumsy installation of the Vickers-Challenger synchronisation gear and Vickers machine gun.

on 10 October 1915, Second Lt H. Medlicott, flying a Scout from No. 2 Squadron, attacked a German two-seater and saw black smoke pouring from its engine, suggesting that he had damaged it. However, Medlicott was distracted by a second enemy and did not observe his victim's fate. On 12 March 1916, Capt. Allcock of No. 13 Squadron intercepted two Albatros two-seaters but had to break away when he was attacked by an enemy fighter. Meanwhile on 10 April, Second Lts Read and Lord Doune of No. 25 Squadron attacked a Fokker and might easily have brought it down had both not suffered gun jams and abandoned their attacks. Second Lt Albert Ball made his first flight in a Scout, 5316, on 29 April. On 5 May, Ball took 5313, one of No. 11 Squadron's three Scouts, over the lines. He fired a few rounds to warm up his gun but saw no enemy machines and on landing, discovered that the synchronisation gear was not working and had damaged his own propeller. On 15 May 1916, Ball was flying 5313 when he spotted an Albatros reconnaissance machine below, heading towards Beaumont. Ball described what happened in a letter to his sister:

> I was at 12,000 feet and saw a Hun at 5,000. It started off and I went after it, catching up when 20 miles over its own lines. It took 120 shots to do it in, but in the end it went down upside down.

But Ball did not see it crash and could not be credited with a victory; however, the next day, he shot down an Albatros two-seater, wounding the observer to achieve the first of his forty-four confirmed victories. This was to be Ball's only kill in a Scout, the remainder achieved in

The Scout D, the last and most numerous variant of the basic design with a larger rudder and more powerful engine.

An unidentified Scout D showing the modified cowling enclosing its more powerful engine.

either the French-designed Nieuport or the well-known Royal Aircraft Factory S.E.5.

As well as serving on the Western Front, the Scout saw action in other theatres of war, both with the RFC and with the RNAS. The Scout was also employed in the home defence role, examples being stationed at Eastbourne, Dover, Manston, Eastchurch, the Isle of Grain, Chingford, Yarmouth, Cranwell, Scarborough and Redcar. The Scouts, along with other home defence aircraft, scrambled whenever daylight raids by German bombers were reported as well as patrolling in the hope of intercepting enemy airships raiding by night. In this role, the Scout was often armed with canisters of Ranken darts, an incendiary device designed for use against Zeppelins which were carried externally and released when flying above the enemy airship with the intention of penetrating the envelope and igniting the escaping hydrogen. The last home defence mission flown by Scouts was as late as August 1917 when N5390 and 5391, both stationed at Manston, took off in an attempt to catch raiding Gotha bombers attacking London.

On 3 November 1915, the Scout made history when Lt H. F. Towle successfully flew 1255 from the deck of HMS *Vindex*, a former Isle of Man steam packet that had been converted to carry land and seaplanes. Landing back on the ship was not possible and although the seaplane could land alongside and be hoisted aboard, those machines, like the Scout with wheeled undercarriages, were obliged to ditch in the sea. In order to take off from the short flying deck (which was just 64-feet long), the ship steamed at full speed into the wind, the Scout being held in flying position, its tail skid on a special launching trestle that was developed at the Isle of Grain with the aid of another Scout, 3026.

HMS *Vindex* operated mainly in the North Sea and on 2 August 1916, one of its Scouts, 8953, flown by Ft Sub. Lt L. T. Freeman, took off and intercepted Zeppelin *L17*. The Scout managed to climb above the airship and released its Ranken darts and made several passes. A puff of smoke convinced Freeman that he had scored a hit on his final pass although the airship appeared undamaged. However, the Zeppelin was fitted with a defensive machine gun and managed to hit the Scout, causing a fuel leak as a result of which it ditched in the sea. The machine stayed afloat, its forward fuselage under water. Freeman was obliged to climb onto the tail from where, after about an hour and a half, he was rescued by the Belgian cargo ship, *Anver*, and taken to Holland where he was treated as a shipwrecked sailor and released a few days later.

An alternative idea for intercepting raiding airships was to attach a small aeroplane to the upper wing of a larger flying boat (the flying boat's greater endurance increasing the fighter's patrol time considerably). In

A Bristol Scout being prepared for launching from HMS *Vindex* in November 1916 showing the baulks of timber needed to hold it in flying position.

Bristol Scout, 8953, that attacked Zeppelin *L17* seen at Filton after completion. The identity of the man stood alongside is unknown.

May 1916, Scout C, 3028, piloted by Ft Lt M. J. Day, took off while attached to a Porte Baby flown by its designer J. C. Porte. The Scout was successfully released at 1,000 feet, but the idea was not developed further.

The Bristol Scout served in small numbers in Palestine with the RFC's Nos 14, 67 (Australian) and 111 Squadrons, with at least one example remaining in active use until October 1917. No. 67 Squadron, which was later renamed 1 Squadron Australian Flying Corps, was issued with three Scout Cs to add to its mixture of aircraft and assigned one to each flight as escorts; however, they were considered poor climbers and the Martinsyde G100 'Elephant' was preferred by the Australian pilots. The Scouts were therefore returned to the depot after a three-month trial.

In April 1917, when No. 30 Squadron in Mesopotamia requested fighter aircraft to defend their reconnaissance/bombing machines against a new German fighter, they were sent Bristol Scouts from the depot in Egypt. On 22 April, one of these flown by Lt M. L. Maguire, shot down an enemy Halberstadt over Istabulat. No. 63 Squadron, another Army co-operation unit serving in Mesopotamia, also had a few Bristol Scouts on strength, the remainder of its aircraft being R.E.8 reconnaissance machines. No. 47 Squadron, based at Salonika and operating on the Macedonian Front, also included a few Bristol Scouts such as C3037 and C3040 in its assortment of aircraft.

Many Scouts ended up in training establishments, both in the UK and overseas, including the RNAS Flying School at Vendôme, although in many cases their availability to student pilots was limited as senior officers liked to adopt them as personal transports. One example, A1789—that served with the Central Flying School at Upavon, then at London Colney and finally at Hounslow—underwent numerous changes to its markings. Initially fitted with a 100-hp Gnome engine, it was then powered with a 110-hp Clerget and reverted to the Gnome with a propeller spinner being added and then removed. A single example, 8926, went to Australia and shipped on the SS *Bakara* in the summer of 1916 and served at the Flying School at Point Cook, near Melbourne, where it was considered 'too advanced' for use by student pilots. 8926 was therefore reserved, as in the UK, for instructors to fly.

B763, a SARD rebuild, found its way to the USA and was based at McCook Field, and moved to Wright Field in April 1921.

5570 survived the war and was sold to a private owner, Major J. A. McKelvie, who had served with No. 62 Squadron, joining the civil register as G-EAGR. In 1926, it was sold to Sqn Ldr H. V. Champion de Crespigny who had flown the type with No. 11 Squadron in 1916, but sold it the following year when he was posted to India. It became the property of Ft Lt A. M. Wray until it was scrapped at South Cave in 1933.

MARTINSYDE S1

H. P. Martin and G. H. Handasyde, who were both formerly connected with the car industry, joined forces in 1908. After at least one false start, they began the construction of a series of graceful monoplanes loosely based on the French 'Antoinette' that came close to beating Blériot in the race to cross the English Channel. These machines soon became known as Martinsydes and had a reputation for being well engineered and soundly constructed. During 1914 and no doubt inspired by the success of the S.E.2 and Sopwith Tabloid, the company abandoned the monoplane in favour of a compact biplane design of which was carried out by A. A. ('Tony') Fletcher who had joined the company after serving an apprenticeship with Handley Page. Although eventually designated the S1, as progress with its construction was recorded in *Flight* magazine, it was never referred to as anything but a fast scout. Emerging from the workshops a few weeks after the beginning of the war, the machine was powered by an 80-hp Gnome rotary engine enclosed in a bull-nose cowling similar to that of the first Sopwith Tabloid. The wings were staggered and employed single-bay bracing with streamlined Rafwires, all four wings provided with ailerons to provide efficient control in roll while a few degrees of dihedral ensured stability. The fuselage was flat sided with a triangular decking, tapering neatly to a rather elegant low-aspect-ratio fin and rudder inherited from its monoplane predecessors. The forward fuselage was covered with plywood and the metal fittings were of perforated steel plate in the manner favoured by Fletcher. However, the most unusual feature was its undercarriage where two small nose wheels were mounted on the forward tips of the skids, ahead of the two main wheels giving it a practical but cumbersome appearance.

Tests revealed that the Martinsyde was rather unstable fore and aft, and that aileron response was poor given the size of the controls surfaces. These faults were evidently not considered serious as during September, the Martinsyde was impressed into the RFC where it was given the serial 696. Its makers were paid £1,050 and the Martinsyde was assigned to No. 1 Squadron that was then reforming as an aeroplane unit after giving up airship operations. Anticipating that further examples would be required, Martin and Handasyde began construction in advance of receipt of an official order and were thus able to deliver about a dozen

An early Martinsyde S1, 599, showing the practical but rather cumbersome four-wheeled undercarriage that spoiled its otherwise very trim lines.

more before the end of the year with a total of sixty being built. Later examples had a simple vee undercarriage of more conventional design and this was fitted to some of the earlier machines. Armament, when fitted, comprised a drum-fed machine gun mounted on the top wing. Its top speed was 87 mph, faster than many contemporary two-seaters, but slower than rival designs powered by the same engine.

1601, the first example to go to France, joined No. 5 Squadron on 5 January 1915. This was followed by 749 two days later and on 10 January, No. 6 Squadron received 748. At this time, there were no specialist fighter or bomber squadrons. At the opening of the Battle of Neuve Chapelle on 10 March 1915, No. 5 Squadron was assigned the task of bombing a railway junction just north of Menin Station to hinder the transport of reinforcement troops. The commanding officer thought the squadron's Martinsydes were best suited to the job as it could lift a 100-lb bomb. Only three pilots had flown the Martinsyde and the two lightest aviators tossed a coin, Capt. George Carmichael thus being selected. Carmichael managed to climb to 4,000 feet, out of range of small-arms fire from the ground, before crossing the lines, but dived down to about 100 feet to make his attack, following the railway tracks and sighting through a hole in the cockpit floor. Remarkably,

The simplified undercarriage improved the appearance of the S1. Also visible in this photograph of 5452 is the large cut-out in the trailing edge of the upper-centre section to improve the pilot's view.

Carmichael hit his target perfectly but before climbing away, he passed over a large mass of German soldiers, his machine sustaining a number of bullet holes before he could escape and return to base.

No. 6 Squadron received a second S1 by 17 March to help chase away enemy aeroplanes that were interfering with their patrols. On 10 May, Louis Strange was flying 2449 on such a duty and having attacked an Aviatik two-seater without result, broke off to change the ammunition drum on his Lewis gun. The drum failed to release and so Strange stood up in the cockpit, holding the control column between his knees to get a better grip. However, the machine flipped over, throwing him out of the cockpit and entered a flat spin. Strange managed to hold on to one of the centre-section struts and later recalled:

> I kept on kicking upwards behind me until at last I got one foot, and then the other, hooked inside the cockpit. Somehow I got the stick between my legs again and jammed on full elevator and aileron. I do not know exactly what happened then, but the trick was done. The

machine came the right way up and I fell off the top plane and into my seat with a bump.

Strange managed to return to No. 6 Squadron's airfield where his commanding officer reprimanded him for the loss of his seat cushion and causing unnecessary damage, most of his instruments having been wrecked. Only a handful of other examples served on the Western Front with Nos 1 and 4 Squadrons having one or two each for escort duties. The Martinsyde was never a popular machine as the ailerons were not particularly effective and it was reported to be rather unstable fore and aft.

By August 1915, Nos 1, 4, 5 and 6 Squadrons had returned their Martinsydes to the depot and yet on 14 September, 2823 was issued to No. 12 Squadron although it did not remain in use for long, being struck off charge on 1 October and ending the type's career in France.

Back in the UK with Zeppelin raids proving a threat to civilian morale, on 6 May 1915, airfields around London—including Brooklands, Farnborough, Hounslow, Joyce Green and Northolt as well as those at Dover and Shoreham—were instructed to keep at least one aircraft in readiness to defend the capital against attack. The Martinsyde S1 was amongst the types recommended for the role and was intended to be armed with six carcass bombs (incendiary devices which were dropped through a tube and fused as they fell), three powder bombs, twelve Hales grenades and 150 Ranken darts. The War Office further instructed that there was 'no advantage' in the machines carrying a machine gun. Pilots doubted the machine's ability to carry such a load and a trial revealed that when fully armed, the S1 took almost 22 minutes to climb to 6,000 feet and would be unlikely to reach the Zeppelin's operating altitudes of up to twice this height. After a number of valiant but abortive sorties had been flown, the War Office declared on 29 October 1915 that the Martinsydes were unsuited to the role.

The summer of 1915 saw four S1s, including 4343, 4244 and 4250, sent to the Middle East with 4244 joining No. 30 Squadron based at Basrah in Mesopotamia (now Iraq) on 26 August. Piloted by Major H. L. Reilly, its reconnaissance missions provided all the information General Charles Townsend needed for the first battle of Kut, a small town besieged by Ottoman forces. On 6 October and flown by Capt. H. A. Petre, 4244 carried out the first reconnaissance of Baghdad. Careers of the other machines were less significant. Opportunities for aerial combat were few and their reconnaissance missions less noteworthy. 4243 crashed and was written off on 13 September, the remaining two

Martinsyde S1, 2449, that served with No. 4 Squadron at St Omer. It is finished in a primitive camouflage and its only national markings being a small Union Jack on the rudder.

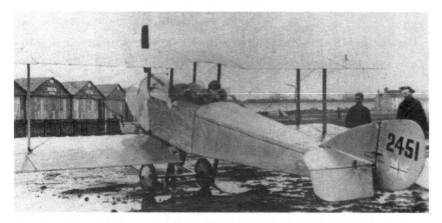

Martinsyde S1, 2451, seen with No. 2 Reserve Squadron at Brooklands.

A line-up of aircraft in the desert with two S1s nearest to the camera. The second has its engine covered to protect it from sand.

An unidentified Martinsyde S1 at a training unit. The aircraft in the background is an Avro 504. (*Cross & Cockade Collection*)

Martinsydes not surviving much longer as they were also destroyed, therefore ending the S1's career as a scout.

Four examples went to training establishments upon their acceptance by the RFC in 1914 with a further forty joining them during 1915. These machines acted as advanced trainers until they were superseded by more state of the art designs later in the war.

ROYAL AIRCRAFT FACTORY S.E.4A

The S.E.4 was built during the first half of 1914 to be the fastest aeroplane in the world. Designed by Henry Folland, it was powered by a 160-hp two-row Gnome rotary engine and based loosely on the S.E.2 with wings of similar area and planform, but with every possible aeronautical refinement to reduce resistance and so increase speed. Bracing wires were streamlined Rafwires and just one broad strut was fitted between each pair of wings, its ends flared to an 'I' shape to attach to each wing spar, the fixing bolts flush with the finished surface. It was covered with a Ramie fabric that was lighter than the usual linen and the gaps between control surfaces were covered with a material described as 'fine elastic mesh'. The engine was fully cowled and the hub of the large four-blade propeller was fitted with a conical spinner. As a final refinement to further reduce drag, a cockpit canopy of moulded celluloid was designed and, not without difficulty, was duly made. However, it was never used as pilots complained that it distorted their view.

The original undercarriage comprised a transverse leaf spring mounted at the apex of an inverted tripod of struts, but proved to roll excessively when taxiing and a more conventional vee undercarriage was substituted before an attempted take-off. Thus modified, it first flew piloted by Norman Spratt in July 1914 and, when officially timed, recorded a top speed of 134.5 mph.

Although adopted by the RFC at the outbreak of war and assigned the serial number 628, it never entered service as on 12 August while it was still at the Royal Aircraft Factory, the starboard wheel collapsed on landing and the machine somersaulted, landing on its back and was damaged beyond repair. Almost immediately, work began on the design of a successor that was intended to be more serviceable and have a lower-powered engine. Also, it was to possess a lower landing speed than the 52 mph of the S.E.4 while being as fast as possible. The completed design, again by Henry Folland, had little in connection with the S.E.4, but was nonetheless designated as the S.E.4a, perhaps to fool the enemy to believe that it would be equally fast (this was unlikely as it was powered by an 80-hp Gnome rotary engine). Unlike its predecessor, the S.E.4a was designed to be stable as well as manoeuvrable and its staggered wings were given a fairly generous 3½ degrees of dihedral to ensure lateral stability.

Full-span ailerons were fitted to all four wings and as in the S.E.4, lowered together by means of a hand crank to act as landing flaps. They could also be reflexed upwards, reducing the wing camber and thus the drag when flying fast. There was no upper-centre section, the two wings being joined on the aircraft's centreline and supported on a cabane structure that formed two inverted vees viewed from ahead. The fuselage was the usual wire-braced box section that was fabric covered, but with the addition of a tapered headrest fairing that enhanced the machine's streamlined appearance. The undercarriage was the now usual two inverted vees of steel tube faired with wood to a streamlined section and with the axle bound to their apexes with rubber shock cord. The sprung tailskid was mounted on the bottom of the sternpost and covered with a fairing that formed a ventral fin, a design later adopted for the S.E.5.

The S.E.4 as first built with the innovative but impractical sprung undercarriage and conical propeller spinner.

The S.E.4 fitted with the vee undercarriage that enabled it to successfully take off.

Before the machine was completed, volume production was expected as on 3 May 1915, the Assistant Director of Military Aeronautics wrote to the officer commanding the admin wing of the RFC:

> I am to inform you that for purposes of official nomenclature, the Royal Aircraft Factory designed machines F.E.2b and S.E.4 (sic) now being put out to contract will be known as 'Fighter Mk1' and 'Scout Mk1' respectively, and will be referred to as such in all communications concerning them.

However, no contract for the manufacture of the S.E.4a was placed. The four examples built by the Royal Aircraft Factory and given the serial numbers 5609–5612 were the only examples produced. The first machine completed, 5609, had its fuselage fully faired with formers and stringers continuing the circular shape of the engine cowling for the entire length of the fuselage. A large spinner was fitted to the propeller hub, its diameter almost as great as that of the cowling with a small hole at its apex to admit air to the engine. The stub spars, to which the

S.E.4a, 5609, seen on Farnborough Common. There is a mounting for a Lewis gun on the upper-centre section although no gun is fitted.

lower wings were attached, were faired to an aerofoil section and the cables operating the ailerons were routed internally through the wings. Provision was made for mounting a Lewis gun on the upper wing that fired over the propeller tips. Completed and ready for its final inspection on 23 June 1915, it made its first flight and piloted by Frank Goodden two days later.

Subsequent machines were finished more simply with semi-conical fairings blending the curve of the engine cowling into the flat fuselage sides with the stub spars uncovered to provide some downward view from the cockpit and with the ailerons cables, guides and pulleys exposed for ease of maintenance.

5611 was retained by the Royal Aircraft Factory and tested with both the Le Rhône and Clerget 80-hp rotary engines as well as the Gnome. Its full-span ailerons were tested both as landing flaps, reducing the landing speed from 45 mph to 40 mph. Reflexed upwards, the reduction in drag adding just 2 mph to the machine's top speed of around 90 mph. It was generally considered that these improvements did not fully justify the weight and complication of the apparatus needed to achieve them,

S.E.4a, 5611, in flight. (*P. F. Wright*)

but they remained a feature of the design.

Frank Goodden seemed to like the machine and occasionally performed aerobatics over the Farnborough airfield to the delight of staff.

5610, which was completed on 16 July, was first sent to the Central Flying School for evaluation and then fitted with a Lewis gun on its upper wing. It entered RFC service at Joyce Green on Dartford Marshes where it carried out home defence duties attempting to intercept raiding Zeppelins. 5612 also joined the RFC on home defence duties and was stationed at Hounslow. In the morning of 24 September, it was flown by Captain Bindon Blood. (A descendant of Thomas Blood aka 'Captain Blood' who attempted to steal the crown jewels in 1672.) Blood took 5612 up again in the afternoon, but attempted to turn too sharply and the machine stalled and spun to the ground. The petrol tank burst, engulfing the machine in flames with Blood sustaining injuries from which he died the following day.

The fate of the remaining three machines appears to be unrecorded.

VICKERS ES1

Just after the start of the war, Harold Barnwell—recently appointed chief test pilot at Vickers after the closure of the company's flying school at which he had been an instructor—devised a fast scout known unofficially as the Barnwell Bullet. However, it appears that more than the name was unofficial as Barnwell is alleged to have completed the machine without official authority, even obtaining its engine, a 100-hp Gnome Monosoupape, from the company's stores at Erith by clandestine means. Unfortunately, Barnwell's skill as a pilot was not matched with similar skill as a designer and the machine overturned on its attempt to take off, the undercarriage collapsing. However, it did show sufficient potential for the company to take it over assigning the necessary reconfiguration that included a more robust undercarriage with a wider track and larger wheels. The design team, led by Rex Peirson, also modified the tail surfaces. Named the Experimental Scout No.1 or ES1, it was almost entirely conventional both in layout and construction. Its only unusual feature was that the Gnome engine was enclosed in a full cowling of unusually deep chord with a narrow slot to admit cooling air. Also, the fuselage was faired round to match the shape of the cowling, maintaining a constant diameter to a point aft of the cockpit, producing a streamlined shape like an elongated teardrop. When first completed in August 1915, its single-bay wings had square cut tips with no stagger, the cockpit placed between them. The pilot's head was located under the rear spar limiting his view upwards while the downward view was restricted both by the lower wing and bulged fuselage sides.

During September, King George V paid a visit to Vickers at Crayford, and accompanied by a number of dignitaries, was shown the ES1. Test flying clearly revealed some deficiency in control as by November its wings had been modified, increasing the size of the ailerons and rounding off the tips. On test, it attained the impressive speed of around 115 mph and was claimed by Vickers to be the first aeroplane able to gain height while performing a loop. Barnwell flew the ES1 to Hendon on 6 November 1915 causing something of a sensation by appearing at high speed, performing several climbing loops, and then departing, the incident being widely reported in the aviation press.

Speed trials conducted on 8 November recorded an improved top speed of 118 mph and was considered that 'the machine would out climb any existing known type of aircraft', although the test report also stated 'her great drawback is the very small field of view afforded to the pilot. He can see very little above and nothing down below.' However, its high

Preparing the prototype Vickers ES1 for take-off showing the original square wing tips. (*Eric Harlin*)

The original Vickers ES1 over Hendon where its remarkable performance impressed the gathered crowds.

speed appears to have been sufficient compensation for the poor view and the ES1 was sent to France for evaluation, arriving at St Omer on 27 December 1915. It was here that it was realised that the little scout had not been given a serial number. Therefore, it was assigned the number 5127, one of a batch reserved for aeroplanes in France. Not only was the view from the cockpit severely criticised—it being necessary to put the machine into a steep bank in order to get a view of the ground below—but it was also found that if the engine mixture controls were not adjusted with care, unused fuel would collect at the bottom of the cowling and ignite. Several such fires occurred much to the consternation of the pilots involved, although without significant damage.

On 5 January, an ES1 was crashed by Capt. Playfair, an experienced Bristol Scout pilot; however, the aircraft was not badly damaged and was repaired for flight a few days later. On 10 January 1916, Lt-Col. Brooke-Popham, then a senior staff officer in France, wrote to the Assistant Director of Military Aeronautics explaining that he considered the machine dangerous due to the risk of fire and that he had given orders for all future flights to be cancelled. On 23 January, the ADMA agreed and it was returned to England, dismantled and packed in a crate.

Yet this was not the end of the ES1 for a further six examples, 7509 and 7756-7760, were built on contract 87/A/344, the serials being allotted on 18 February 1916. These machines differed slightly from the original and were therefore designated ES1 Mk II, although the designation ES2 appears to have been occasionally used. The fire risk was reduced, if not entirely eliminated, by forming an aperture in the bottom of the cowling through which surplus petrol could be drained. The wing bracing was changed from cable to streamlined Rafwires and most importantly, a Vickers machine gun—synchronised by the newly invented Vickers-Challenger mechanical gear—was fitted into a recess on the portside of the fuselage decking. The machine gun was located close to the centre-section struts, bullets exiting through a hole in the engine cowling. The ES1 was amongst the first designs to be fitted with this synchronisation gear, the first to enter British service and was almost certainly involved in the gear's development (to which individual aeroplane it was first fitted is uncertain). 7759 was fitted with a large and clear view panel in the centre section. The type was officially known as the Vickers Scout, although it was occasionally referred to as the Bullet.

Two examples, 7509 and 7756, were tested by the Central Flying School and fitted with alternative engines as well as the Gnome—7509 having the 110-hp Clerget and 7756 a similarly rated Le Rhône. Neither showed any advantage as despite the increase in horsepower, the machine was fastest when fitted with the Gnome. The CFS report on handling the ES1 stated that it was 'tiring to fly' and 'required great care when landing' as well as criticising the view from the cockpit. 7756

The rather portly shape of the ES1 as well as the restricted view from the cockpit clearly shown in 7509, the first of a small production run.

was also found to be tail heavy, possibly because the Le Rhône engine was lighter than the Gnome for which it had been designed. Despite its impressive top speed, these comments were sufficient to condemn the design and no further production orders were placed, although the examples ordered found some use by the RFC. Its testing completed, 7756 was flown out to No. 1 depot at St Omer by Maj. J. E. Tennant on 18 May 1916 and assigned to No. 11 Squadron, presumably as an escort as the squadron was in the process of converting from the Vickers FB5 to the Royal Aircraft Factory F.E.2b. The original machine, 5127, which was now fitted with a synchronised machine gun, went to France with No. 32 Squadron, along with its DH2s on 28 May. 7758 was also flown on occasion by Major L. W. B. Rees while 7757 served with No. 70 Squadron that was otherwise equipped with the two-seat Sopwith 1½ Strutter joining 'A' Flight on 24 May.

The ES1 only remained in service for a few weeks as it was declared to be 'of no military value' largely due to the lack of view from the cockpit. 7756 was returned to No. 2 depot at Candas on 7 June when it was reported to be in a poor condition; however, it would appear to have survived until January 1917 when it was believed to have been wrecked. 5127 was last recorded with No. 32 Squadron on 7 June 1916, its fate unrecorded. 7758 had been returned to No. 1 depot by 22 June when the engine, gun and synchronisation gear were removed for reuse. 7757 was returned to the UK by the end of June.

Not being required in France, 7509, 7759 and 7760 went to No. 50 (Home Defence) Squadron that operated a mixture of aeroplanes from various bases in Kent. The ES1 proved fairly popular with pilots as its high speed gave it a reasonable chance of intercepting enemy raiders, although none appears to have done so. 5127, which had returned from France, also went to No. 50 Squadron and survived until 23 March 1917 when it made a forced landing while being flown from its base at Bekesbourne to Farnborough. Also based at Bekesbourne, 7759 remained active through the summer of 1917 and pursued day raiders on 25 May, 5 June and 13 June, piloted by Capt. A. J. Capel and by 2 Lt I. M. Davis on 4 July. Its final recorded sortie was on 7 July and the pilot's name was unrecorded.

ROYAL AIRCRAFT FACTORY B.E.12

In the spring of 1915 before the advent of the Fokker monoplane and its synchronised machine gun, the mainstay of the RFC, the Royal Aircraft Factory's B.E.2c two-seat reconnaissance machine, was marred only by its low power. As its creators noted, the B.E.2c was often flown solo for photographic or bombing missions and its performance marginally increased when released from the additional weight of an observer. In May, work began on a single-seat version fitted with a more powerful engine that could carry out these essential tasks more effectively.

The prototype, later designated B.E.12, was created by the conversion of a standard production B.E.2c, 1697, which had been built by the British and Colonial Aeroplane Company. As originally built, 1697 was an early model powered by a 70-hp V8 Renault engine rather than the 90-hp RAF1a that had superseded it. Also, it was fitted with a twin-skid undercarriage, both of which were removed and returned to the stores as spares during June. The engine mounting was modified to accept the 140-hp V12 RAF4a engine. The increased length eliminated the forward cockpit and was fitted with two small air scoops in tandem with a complex exhaust system that terminated in a single vertical discharge on the engine centreline. A fuel tank, shaped to match the fuselage decking, was fitted behind the engine and a vee undercarriage that was introduced to the B.E.2c was fitted. The wings and tail surfaces remained as originally designed.

Conversion work proceeded through June and July but on the morning of 28 July, the B.E.12 was submitted for final inspection with a request that it should be treated as urgent. Approval was given later the same day and in the evening it making its first flight with Mervyn O'Gorman, the Factory Superintendent, writing to Col. W. S. Brancker, then Director of Air Organisation, as follows:

> I have had a preliminary run on B.E.12 today. As I think you know, a Maurice Farman alighted on my speed box on the speed course and smashed it up, but I can say that she is as stable as B.E.2c—alights as slowly—climbs like mad and flies in the neighbourhood of 100 mph. I do not see why pilots who can fly a B.E.2c should not use it as soon as they get it. They can throttle down at first so that it is a B.E.2c and after a few alightings, open up the throttle.

1697 was not as good as O'Gorman initially believed as it remained at Farnborough for further development. Throughout the summer, engineers were largely concerned in adequately cooling the rear cylinders of the V12 engine and by 22 September, it had been fitted with an enlarged fin. The first production order, 87/A/123, for fifty machines (6136–6185) was placed with the Standard Motor Company on 30 September with an order for 200 (6478–6677) placed with the Daimler Company shortly thereafter. Both of these companies were based

The prototype B.E.12, 1697, its exhaust pipes joined into a single vertical outlet.

in Coventry and production was also undertaken by the Coventry Ordnance Works. Production machines differed from the original in having modified engine mountings, a single and larger air scoop above the engine, and the top of the petrol tank was shaped to blend the angle of the scoop into the line of the fuselage decking. Separate exhausts were fitted to each cylinder bank, discharging above the upper wing, and the design reverted to the B.E.2c-style triangular fin originally fitted to 1697. A camera mounting was included as a standard fitting on the starboard side of the fuselage outside the cockpit.

Both Daimler and Siddeley-Deasy Ltd, another Coventry-based company, built the RAF4a engine with the latter company delivering their first completed engine in December 1915 (deliveries from Daimler commenced in February 1916). However, Daimler was the first to deliver a completed B.E.12 with 6478 handed over towards the end of March 1916. It was sent to the Central Flying School for evaluation on 3 April where it was joined by 6479 on 11 May and received the following report:

Stability, lateral and longitudinal, good. Directional bad with small fin.

The first B.E.12 completed by Daimler, its serial, 6478, has been marked on the fin ready to be painted.

> Length of run to unstuck 140 yards. To pull up with engine stopped 230 yards. Machine was not tiring to fly. Lands as easily as B.E.2c. Manoeuvres slower than B.E.2c. Larger fin required.

Meanwhile at Farnborough with the Fokker Scourge on going and with a growing need to arm British aeroplanes, some effort was being made to fit a gun to the B.E.12. However, the air scoop and exhaust were proving a hindrance as the gun could not be fitted in front of the pilot. Also, a further problem was the lack of suitable synchronisation gear. 1697 was therefore first fitted with a Lewis gun, mounted on the portside of the fuselage and with deflector blocks fitted to the propeller to prevent damage. Introduction of the Vickers-Challenger mechanical gear saved the day and allowed a belt-fed Vickers machine gun to be fitted in place of the Lewis. This was mounted on the portside of the fuselage, thus avoiding the engine's air scoop and also simplified the installation of the mechanical linkage for the synchronisation gear. Sighting was still an issue due to the protruding air scoop and a ring and bead-sight system was therefore fitted on the outside of the port interplane struts. This forced the pilot to lean out into the slipstream to take aim, a far from ideal arrangement, but all that was possible on a machine that had never been designed to be armed.

Deflector blocks fitted to the prototype B.E.12's propeller to allow a forward-firing Lewis gun to be fitted.

The armament first adopted comprised of a Vickers gun mounted on the portside of the fuselage with the operating rod of the Vickers-Challenger synchronisation gear visible below it. A Strange mounting, for a rearward-firing Lewis gun, is fitted behind the cockpit.

Tests were also conducted with the Davis gun that inclined upwards for operations against Zeppelins whose raids were creating havoc among the civilian population. This weapon fired a two-lb shell and was made recoilless by ejecting a similar weight of lead shot and grease backwards through an opposed barrel. In turn, this was fired by the same charge and the breech was central between both barrels. Invented in 1910, the Davis gun was a modest success; however, its installation on the B.E.12 was not and the experiment was quickly discontinued.

The B.E.12 first entered service in the home defence role with 6484 joining No. 52 Squadron on 18 May with 6489 going to No. 51 Squadron. 6490 was sent to No. 53 Squadron and others quickly followed.

6479 and 6483 were the first examples to go to France, the latter joining No. 10 Squadron on 31 May and made its first operational sortie as an escort piloted by the squadron's commanding officer, Major W. Mitchell. When flown as a fighter, its poor manoeuvrability was immediately apparent as was the inherent stability that was part of its design as a reconnaissance machine (inherited from the B.E.2c). At the

A4042 appears to be preparing for take-off. It served with several training units in the UK and crashed on Streatham Common on 29 April 1917 killing its pilot, Lt P. N. Clark. (*P. H. T. Green Collection*)

end of June, Col. H. R. M. Brooke-Popham, the RFC's Quartermaster, complained that 'The pilot cannot exert enough force on the elevators to keep the machine's nose down completely preventing a suitable dive with the engine at full throttle.' This problem was later resolved by exchanging the tailplane and elevators for the smaller surfaces designed for the B.E.2e. Brooke-Popham also passed on a complaint that the synchronisation gear would not operate the gun if the engine speed fell below 800 rev/min. This happened quite often during manoeuvres and Brooke-Popham suggested that the gear be fitted with a double cam that resolved the problem.

No. 19 Squadron, which had first formed in 1915, was fully equipped with the B.E.12 in June 1916 and flew to France the following month. They arrived at the depot at St Omer on 30 July before flying on to their base at Fienvillers that they were to share with No. 27 Squadron the next day. The B.E.12 was still not an effective fighter and the squadron suffered its first casualty on 13 August when 6349, flying as an escort, was brought down by a German two-seater and captured intact, its pilot, 2 Lt C. Geen, taken prisoner.

No. 21 Squadron, the only other unit to be fully equipped with the B.E.12, converted to the type from the R.E.7 bomber towards the end of August. Although its duties now included defensive patrols, it continued to operate in the bombing role with up to 336-lbs of bombs in racks under the lower wings. In this role, it was sometimes fitted with a rearward-facing Lewis gun mounted on the portside of the fuselage for defence of the tail and sighting the weapon was almost impossible and at least one pilot considered it 'little more than a joke'. However, on 22 September 1916, Lt G. A. Baker of No. 19 Squadron while flying 6548 shot down an enemy aircraft—one of three victories achieved by the squadron. This was a number that far exceeded those lost due to engine failure or enemy action and two days later, Brig-Gen. Hugh Trenchard, commander of the RFC in France, wrote 'I have come to the conclusion that the B.E.12 aeroplane is not a fighting machine in any way.' He requested that no more be sent to France and those already there should be replaced as soon as practicable.

The introduction of the B.E.2e with single-bay wings of unequal span improved the performance of the reconnaissance machine sufficiently and it was logical that wings of the same design should be tried on its descendant, the B.E.12. Designated as the B.E.12a, orders for the new

An immaculately finished production B.E.12, 6536, built by Daimler and fitted with bomb rails below the lower wings.

variant were placed with Daimler and the Coventry Ordnance Works, both for fifty machines. Although slightly faster than the original with two-bay wings and considered easier to land when tested at the CFS in May 1917, the RFC in France found it offered no improvement in such essential elements as manoeuvrability and none entered service. Instead, they were assigned to home defence units, training establishments, and to squadrons operating in the Middle East where conditions were considered less demanding than those in France.

In Salonika, No. 47 Squadron received its first B.E.12s in October 1916. The squadron was never equipped with any one type, but like most units in the region, operated a variety of machines, both single and two-seaters. No. 17 Squadron, also operating in Salonika, acquired its first B.E.12s the following month. The idea of sending the B.E.12 to the region seems to have been justified as the type met with some modest success there.

2 Lt C. H. Denning of No. 47 Squadron while flying a B.E.12 managed to bring down an Albatros two-seater on 17 January 1917 that was captured with only slight damage by forces on the ground. Denning shot down another enemy aircraft just two days later. Capt. W. Bell also achieved a number of combat victories flying the B.E.12, including an unidentified enemy aircraft on 24 December 1916 and a Halberstadt fighter on 5 June 1917. Meanwhile, 2 Lt F. D. Travers shot down an Albatros DIII fighter while flying an escort mission on 19 December 1917. Capt. G. W. Murlis-Green of No. 17 Squadron achieved five combat victories flying the B.E.12, including three two-seaters and a seaplane. However, his greatest triumph came on 4 January 1917 when he shot down an Albatros DV fighter that was captured intact.

A single B.E.12 found its way to No. 67 (Aus) Squadron—a unit considered by its personnel to be No. 1 Squadron, Australian Flying Corps, as which it was later officially recognised—then serving in Palestine and was joined in March 1917 by a number of B.E.12as. The Australians greeted the new arrival with some derision, considering them to be 'of no practical use' but, just as typically, did their best with them. On 25 June, while flying as escort to a B.E.2c reconnaissance machine, Lt J. S. Brasell encountered three enemy Fokkers and, although outnumbered and hopelessly outclassed, managed to shoot one down. However, even in the desert, things did not always go so well for the squadron's B.E.12as and on 8 July, Lt C. H. Vaughn was shot down and killed while escorting a B.E.2e and a Martinsyde when they were attacked by two Albatros fighters.

On 4 August, Lt R. M. Smith was flying B.E.12a, A6329, on a bombing mission near Shario when he encountered two enemy aircraft, forcing down a two-seater before turning on its escort. In the ensuing dogfight, a bullet passed through Smith's cheeks and destroyed a number of teeth before Smith emerged victorious. During a photographic reconnaissance in B.E.12a, A575, on 17 January 1918, Lt L. T. Taplin was attacked by an Albatros fighter; however, just twenty rounds from his Vickers gun proved sufficient to shoot it down before he calmly returned to his photography.

During February and March 1918, No. 1 Squadron AFC converted to the Bristol F2b and handed its B.E.12as to No. 142 Squadron at its base at Mejdel. As was usual in the Middle East, the squadron operated an assortment of aeroplanes, mostly for bombing and reconnaissance for which the B.E.12 had originally been intended. B.E.12a, 6610, of No. 37 Squadron achieved the type's most publicised success when on the night of 16/17 June 1917 and piloted by Lt L. P. Watkins, it was credited with the destruction of the Zeppelin raider, *L48*, which crashed in flames at Holly Tree Farm near Theberton in Suffolk. On landing, Watkins submitted the following report of his attack:

> On the morning of June 17th 1917, I was told by Major Hargrave there was a Zeppelin in the vicinity of Harwich and I was ordered to go up in B.E.12, 6610. I climbed to 8,000ft over the aerodrome then struck off in the direction of Harwich still climbing. When at 11,000 ft over Harwich, I saw AA guns firing and several searchlights pointing upwards at the same spot. A minute later, I observed the Zeppelin 2,000 ft above me. After climbing about 500 ft, I fired one drum into its tail but it took no effect. I then climbed to 11,000 ft and fired another drum into its tail without any effect. I then decided to wait until I was at close range before firing another drum. I then climbed steadily until I reached 13,200 ft and was then about 500 ft under the Zeppelin. I fired three bursts of about seven rounds and then the remainder of the drum. The Zepp burst into flames at the tail, the fire running along both sides, then the whole Zepp caught fire and fell burning.

Thousands visited the wreckage and it was widely plundered for souvenirs. It was the last Zeppelin to be brought down over England and Watkins, one of three pilots who had fired at it (the others being Capt. R. H. Saundby who flew a DH2 and Lt Holden and Sgt Ashby in an F.E.2b) were decorated for their efforts.

Despite this success, it had generally been found that the B.E.12 and 12a were unable to climb high enough to reach the latest Zeppelins—which could operate at 20,000 feet—and a number of interceptors were fitted with the 200-hp-geared Hispano-Suiza engine. Being water cooled, this engine did not require the air scoop and so changed the line of the forward fuselage, the fuel tank being fitted reversed so that its sloping top offered less resistance and a frontal radiator introduced. Armament often comprised of two Lewis guns fitted above the upper wing where their muzzle flashes would be out of the pilot's line of sight and so would not adversely affect his night vision, the sights remaining on the centre-section struts. Instrument lighting was provided as were Holt flare brackets on the lower wings to facilitate landing at night and the exhausts usually ended in flame dampers. The conversion was completed by 25 September 1917 and its performance received a fairly enthusiastic report when tested. Despite demand for the Hispano-Suiza engine (particularly for the S.E.5a and Sopwith Dolphin, examples of which were stored awaiting engines), the rate of climb and ceiling of the new variant, designated B.E.12b, was so improved that 100 were ordered from Daimler for home defence duties. However, the Zeppelin raids were largely over and the new engine could not make the B.E.12 a sufficient match for the Gotha bombers then making daylight raids on England.

A total of 601 examples were built, including a further 200 ordered in 1917 for home defence, an overly large number for an aeroplane that

An unidentified B.E.12b fitted with a Lewis gun on the upper-centre section and with a bomb suspended beneath the fuselage. The blank end of the reversed petrol tank projects in front of the windscreen.

Close-up of a B.E.12b powered by a 200-hp Hispano-Suiza and showing the reversed fuel tank. Twin Lewis guns are mounted on the upper-centre section.

Twin Lewis guns fitted to a B.E.12b in the lowered position for reloading. The gun sights are mounted on the starboard-centre section struts.

Guns raised, although not quite into firing position, in which the barrels would be horizontal. The long lever located outside the starboard side of the cockpit is for releasing a bomb. The handling of the starting magneto is on the fuselage side just behind the cockpit.

failed to find its ideal role. At the end of the war, the RAF had around sixty B.E.12 and 12as, mostly in the Middle East. It also possessed over 100 B.E.12bs, most either in store or at various depots, but they seem to have been quickly disposed of as the type saw no post-war use either service or civil.

MARTINSYDE 'ELEPHANT'

The last aeroplane designed by A. A. Fletcher before he left Martinsyde was probably the last aeroplane designed as a high-speed scout. It was designated as the G100, possibly because the engine first considered for it was the six-cylinder 100-hp Green. It was a large machine with a wing span of 38 feet and with its fuel tanks holding just over fifty gallons, the Martinsyde 'Elephant' enjoyed an endurance of 5½ hours so it could scout beyond the range of rival designs. Its wings were staggered, rigging in two bays with neatly raked tips, and all four were fitted with ailerons. A gap was left at the lower wing roots to provide a downward view and each was fitted with a neat plywood endplate. Construction of the attractively tapered fuselage was entirely conventional, but with the ply covering to the forward portion which, together with the perforated metal fittings, was a Fletcher trademark. The low-aspect-ratio fin and rudder were essentially similar to previous Martinsydes and gave the machine, despite its size, a neat, almost graceful appearance. Less graceful was the open-fronted engine cowling fitted to the prototype, 4735, enclosing its 120-hp Beardmore engine (No. 302/WD 1322), a water-cooled six-cylinder inline design modelled on the pre-war Austro-Daimler (the idea of fitting the Green having been abandoned at a very early stage). Each cylinder was fitted with a separate exhaust stub and the radiator was mounted behind the engine with air intakes in the fuselage sides. Unusually, it was fitted with a three-blade wooden propeller built by Lang. The vees of the undercarriage legs were unusually shallow, spanning two fuselage bays instead of the usual one, a feature that added to the machine's rather graceful profile.

Completed in August 1915, 4735 was at the Central Flying School for evaluation by 8 September, moving to Farnborough for adoption by the RFC before the end of the month. On 29 October, it was flown to France where in the depot at St Omer, it was fitted with a replacement engine before being assigned to No. 6 Squadron on 6 November.

An order was placed for a batch of fifty machines (7258–7307) as soon as the prototype had passed its acceptance trials and was followed

The prototype Martinsyde G100 'Elephant', 4735, fitted with a three-blade propeller.

Another view of the prototype G100 showing the elegant low-aspect-ratio fin and rudder, and long tailskid.

by an order for a second batch (7439–7508). Production machines differed from the prototype by having an improved engine cowling with a common exhaust manifold and were fitted with two-blade propellers. The cockpit opening was slightly modified and a camera mounted fitted as standard on the starboard side of the fuselage to facilitate operations in the reconnaissance role. However, by the time it entered service in the spring of 1916, the days of the unarmed scout was over and the G100 was fitted with a Lewis gun on the top wing, offset slightly to starboard of the centreline. The gun mounting comprised of two inverted metal vee shapes, one fixed to the rear spar and braced by a strut to the front spar, the other to which the gun was fitted and hinged at the bottom. With the gun in the firing position, the two vees connected to form a stable mount. Due to the upper wing being located rather high above the pilot, an extended tubular handle was fitted to the gun's spade grip. In order to change ammunition drums, the pilot pressed the release button on the bottom of this handle, pulled the gun down, extended the elastic straps with his right hand, and while almost at full stretch, changed the drum with his left. The elastic straps would then help return the gun to its normal position when the handle was released.

The first production examples began to reach France in early 1916, by which time the German Fokkers were preying on Britain's slower and largely unarmed reconnaissance machines. Therefore, the Martinsydes were issued as escorts, one or two per squadron. Nos 18, 20, 21 and 22 Squadrons each received a few examples, the machine regarded as a fighter where it universally acquired the nickname 'Elephant', perhaps due to its size and wingspan of 38 feet, which made it slightly larger than the B.E.2c two-seaters it was to protect. No. 27 Squadron, the only unit to be fully equipped with the Martinsyde and arrived in France on 1 March 1916, incorporated an elephant into its squadron badge as a result of its long association with the type.

Opinions from pilots flying the Martinsyde varied and Cecil Lewis, a scout pilot who flew one at the depot, recalled many years later:

> The Martinsyde was one of those curiously woolly aeroplanes that a pilot can never get hold of. Owing to the way the weight was slung out along the fuselage, engine, tanks and pilot, it had a very poor turning circle. Only aeroplanes with the weight concentrated were really manoeuvrable.

Yet Oliver Stewart, a former test pilot, had a more tolerant attitude and wrote of it:

A6236 that served with No. 27 Squadron showing the camera mountings on the side of the cockpit.

As a flying machine, the Martinsyde Elephant had many pleasing qualities. It ambled through the air with a rather gentle burbling sound and seemed to get about the country fairly quickly. As for the controls of the Martinsyde Elephant, they were reasonably good although the ailerons failed to produce as quick or as big a response as many pilots would have liked and the elevator had none of the sensitivity of the elevator, for instance, of a Camel. The only serious fault was the poor outlook. The pilot sat just behind the trailing edge of the top plane, with the trailing edge of the lower plane almost immediately below him. Forwards and upwards, a big arc of view was blanked out by the top plane and downwards and forwards there was another big arc of view blanked out. The large chord of the wings added to the blanking effect. In addition, the forward part of the fuselage, and the cowling of the Beardmore engine, came rather high and still further restricted the forward outlook.

Despite its size and alleged lack of manoeuvrability, the Martinsyde 'Elephant' initially met with reasonable success in its adopted role as an escort fighter. On 28 April 1916, 2 Lt S. Dalrymple of No. 27 Squadron engaged and drove off two enemy aircraft while Capt. Cains from the same squadron fired half a drum at a German two-seater. Cains hit the observer and the enemy machine was finished off by Lt Tollemache. Cains and Tollemache scored again on 19 May by shooting down an Albatros two-seater.

However, despite these successes, it was realised that the 'Elephant' was better suited to a different role and on 9 July 1916, it was officially reclassified as a bomber. As such, it could carry a single 230-lb bomb slung beneath the fuselage or an equivalent weight of smaller bombs on racks fitted to the underside of the lower wings. Many were fitted with a second Lewis gun on the portside of the fuselage that allowed the pilot to fire to the rear, although without being able to take proper aim. Pilots, initially at least, continued to have confidence in the type's abilities as a fighter and continued to engage in aerial combat once they had dropped their bombs. For example, on 12 August 1916, 'Elephants' of No. 27 Squadron carried out a bombing raid on the railway east of Valenciennes and on their return journey, shot down an enemy two-seater.

7266 seen at Swingate Downs near Dover served with No. 27 Squadron and was flown by Lt Dalrymple.

The introduction of the German Albatros single-seat fighter in September 1916 changed the fortunes of the Martinsydes and other British machines with loses in combat becoming more frequent. On 23 September, Herbert Bellerby, one of only two sergeant pilots to serve with No. 27 Squadron, became the second victim of a young Manfred von Richthofen when his 'Elephant', 7841, was shot down near Bapaume. 7841 had been one of six aircraft on a bombing mission that was attacked by five Albatros fighters of Jasta 2 and led by ace pilot Oswald Boelcke. A furthermore two Martinsydes flown by 2 Lts E. Roberts and O. Godfrey were also shot down. Lt L. Forbes, who had run out of ammunition, deliberately collided with his attacker, causing it to crash. However, he managed to limp back to the squadron's base despite severe damage to his own machine—testimony to the Martinsyde's construction and strength.

Introduced during 1916, the G102 was externally very similar to the G100, the only difference being the substitution of the uprated 160-hp Beardmore engine in place of the 120-hp version. This gave a small but useful improvement in performance, especially in its lifting capacity in the bombing role, but at the expense of increased fuel consumption that reduced its endurance to just less than 4½ hours. The uprated engine also proved less reliable than the earlier version, but was still very much

Martinsyde 'Elephant', A3978, of No. 27 Squadron that was shot down by Ltn Hess of Jasta 28 on 9 August 1917. Its pilot, 2 Lt W. Skinner, survived to become a prisoner of war.

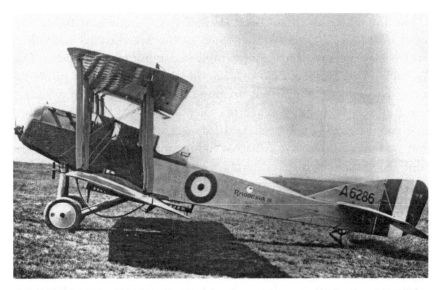

G102, A6286, *Rhodesia III*, showing the three exhaust stubs fitted to its 160-hp Beardmore engine. Like most examples of the type, it is fitted with bomb racks beneath the lower wings.

in demand, especially for the large pusher F.E.2b. Thousands of units were manufactured and competition for deliveries was fierce. The 160-hp engine was usually fitted with three stub exhausts in place of the single manifold of the less powerful type.

Total production was 100 examples of the G100, covered by the two original orders for batches of fifty and 171 G102s, although some of these may have been completed with the less powerful engine when the newer version was not available. Of this total, 125 machines served at one time or another with No. 27 Squadron before it finally converted to the D.H.4 bomber at the beginning of 1918.

An experimental installation of the Sunbeam Arab engine, a water-cooled V8 rated at 150 hp, proved to offer no advantage and was not adopted for production. Experiments were also made with a German-style radiator mounted flush in the upper wing, but gave no obvious benefit and the internal radiator remained standard. In August 1917, A6299 was tested at the Aeroplane Experimental Unit based at Martlesham Heath with an installation of the Eeman gun mounting that comprised of three Lewis guns firing upwards through the centre section for anti-Zeppelin operations in the home defence role. The installation was also tested on a number of other types, including the S.E.5a, but meet with little success, performance being reduced when compared to the standard model and was not adopted for the Martinsyde.

The 'Elephant' also saw action in the Middle East when a total of sixty-four examples were shipped out via the depot in Egypt. Although no squadron was fully equipped with the type, the 'Elephant' served with Nos 14, 67 (Aus) and 142 Squadrons in Palestine and with Nos 30 and 72 Squadrons in Mesopotamia. No. 14 Squadron had at least three 'Elephants' on strength on 5 March 1917, together with five B.E.2cs, a D.H.1, and two Bristol Scouts when they took part in a reconnaissance mission, one of the Martinsydes being piloted by W. E. L. Seward. On 24 March, Seward was again flying a Martinsyde as an escort to a B.E.2c that was to photograph enemy defences when his aircraft was hit by anti-aircraft fire while flying at 8,000 feet near Jaffa. With his engine out of action due to a damaged petrol pipe, Seward had no alternative than to land but chose to do so in the sea, thus avoiding capture by Turkish cavalry and came down about 100 yards offshore near to Ashdod. The aircraft immediately sank and Seward climbed out of his cockpit and began swimming away while under intense rifle fire from the Turks. He stopped to remove his clothing at which point the firing stopped, the Turks presumably believing that they had hit him. A strong and capable swimmer, Seward kept going and swam in a southerly direction for about four hours. Once it was dark, he came ashore naked and began walking following the coast and keeping the sea on his right. Seward had covered

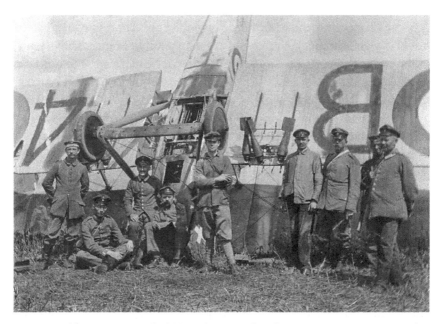

German soldiers posing with A3978 that was shot down on 9 August 1917 and its load of 25-lb Cooper bombs are still fitted.

about 30 miles before being found the next morning by troops from the Wellington Mounted Rifles, a New Zealand unit based near Gaza. Seward was thus able to return to his squadron and resume flying.

No. 14 Squadron formed a small detached flight for special duties in September 1917 that was based near to Akaba on the north-western tip of the Red Sea that included G102, A3957, amongst its assortment of aircraft. Two more 'Elephants', A3958 and A3988, joined the flight in January 1918 and A3999 arrived in May. These machines operated both as fighters and bombers and, as was common for Martinsydes operating in the Middle East, had an additional cross strut bracing the forward legs of the undercarriage, a modification carried out by squadron mechanics and intended to increase its strength for operations on rough terrain. The special duties flight was disbanded at Suez on 23 October 1918, but the fate of its aircraft is unknown.

No. 67 Squadron (1 Squadron AFC) was issued with three G100s at the end of 1916 and as was common practice, assigned one to each of its three flights for escort duties. The Australians frequently referred to the aircraft as Tinsydes, their long range allowing them to bomb far behind the enemy lines. This performance surprised the Turks who believed that they were safe from aerial attack and its pilots confident that they could give good account of themselves if enemy aircraft were encountered. On 20 March 1917, a Martinsyde from the squadron was involved in a courageous rescue with other aircraft when it was engaged in bombing a Turkish supply train. A bomb dropped by the Martinsyde exploded prematurely while just 30 feet below and shrapnel injured its Australian pilot, Lt Francis McNamara, in the upper thigh. As he turned for home, McNamara spotted a B.E.2c on the ground near to the railway and landed beside it. The B.E.2c pilot, Capt. D. W. Rutherford, climbed onto the wing root of the Martinsyde and McNamara attempted to take off, but due to his wound, McNamara could not control the rudder and the machine hit a ditch, destroying its undercarriage. Undeterred and with the Turkish cavalry approaching, the pair made their way to the downed B.E.2c that had suffered some damage, including a burst tyre. McNamara climbed painfully into the pilot's seat while Rutherford swung the propeller, started the engine and climbed into the observer's seat. Although weakened by a loss of blood, McNamara managed to take off and returned to the squadron's base, an act of valour for which he was awarded the Victoria Cross.

In October 1917, No. 67 (Aus) Squadron was issued its first G102 with the 160-hp engine, a total of five joining the squadron. When the squadron converted to the Bristol F2b fighter, its Martinsydes were passed on to No. 142 Squadron that continued to operate a mixture of aircraft types as was common practice in the Middle East. In August, two 'Elephants' from

Martinsyde 'Elephant', A3992, was shot down on 21 August 1917.

7486 the 'Elephant' in which Frank McNammara began the mission during which he earned the Victoria Cross.

No. 72 Squadron saw service at Baku on the Caspian Sea in what is now Azerbaijan. Piloted by Lts M. C. Mackay and R. P. Pope, the two aircraft were set on fire when they became unserviceable, the pilots obliged to continue the war as members of the ground forces. The training unit at Abu Qir, near Alexandria in Egypt, also had the Martinsyde on strength with A3953 among them. No. 30 Squadron in Mesopotamia acquired six G100 'Elephants' during September 1917 while No. 63 Squadron at Basrah, in the south of the region, had a few examples on strength from March 1918. At least two were in use as late as the summer of 1919 with A1584 recorded as flying with No. 63 Squadron on 11 August, the last recorded operational flight of a Martinsyde 'Elephant'.

CHAPTER 2

Pushers and Pulpits

Naturally, given the belligerent nature of mankind in general and of the military in particular, consideration had been given to arming aircraft. However, the concept of aerial combat was new so that designers were unsure of what would be required. At first, it was thought that aeroplanes would need to be armed by having a gun that could be swung in almost any direction to take aim. Performance was considered to be less important than securing a clear view and the widest possible field of fire for it was thought that fighting aeroplanes would seek to engage each other, just as warships of differing classes would do, regardless of any disparity in performance. The idea that the gun could be fixed and that a pilot might aim the gun by flying directly towards his target appears never to have been considered until it arose out of practical experience. Therefore, the first fighters were designed to have a crew of two, the pilot to control the machine and to hold it steady, allowing the second person to aim and fire the gun. And since the gunner required the fullest possible field of fire, the first fighters were pushers with the crew in front and engine and propeller behind. Such an arrangement seems odd to modern eyes, but from the Wright Brothers on, many early aeroplanes were pushers and the general supremacy of the tractor design with the propeller in front had yet to be established. When it was realised that a fighter aircraft needed to be fast, manoeuvrable and preferably a single-seater with a fixed gun, many of the first designs were pushers as the weapon had to be within reach of the pilot. The means of firing ahead and past the spinning propeller of a tractor design had yet to be designed and developed.

The Royal Aircraft Factory's F.E.2 was perhaps the first armed aeroplane with British forces. A pusher machine designed by Geoffrey de Havilland, the F.E.2 visited the Royal Flying Corps' base at Larkhill on Salisbury Plain in August 1912, just a few months after the RFC had come into existence.

The Royal Aircraft Factory's F.E.2 as it appeared during August 1912 armed with a Maxim-type machine gun crudely mounted in the nose.

The aircraft was temporarily fitted with a Maxim-type machine gun mounted fairly crudely in the front of the cockpit. As a pusher, the gun was placed on the nose of the F.E.2 and since its mounting was designed to allow the weapon to swivel, it gave an excellent field of fire stretching from one horizon to the other. This gun installation made a memorable impression on the minds of aeroplane designers and influenced their thinking as the F.E.2 became one of the most successful fighter/bombers of the early war years. It was therefore no surprise that such an armed arrangement inspired a number of other less well remembered designs, some of which entered service and are described in the following pages.

VICKERS FB5 ('GUNBUS')

On 19 November 1912, the Admiralty placed an order with one of its favoured armaments contractors, Vickers, Son & Maxim, who had opened an aviation department the previous year, for a 'fighting aeroplane armed with a machine gun', presumably intending it to be employed in the defence of its shore bases. It seems probable that development of the new machine was already underway at the time of the Admiralty order and that the decision by Vickers to initiate the project had been influenced by the F.E.2.

The new machine designed by A. R. Low was of a pusher configuration and given the type number 18. Its two bay wings were of unequal span and were heavily staggered, the slope of the interplane struts being repeated in those separating the tail booms. Lateral control was by warp and the undercarriage comprised of two wheels mounted on half axles with a central skid. The nacelle had a framework of steel tubing and was covered in aluminium alloy sheeting. Power was provided by a water-cooled V8 Wolseley engine rated at 80 hp and a Vickers belt-fed machine gun was fitted in the nose of the nacelle where it enjoyed a 60 degree cone of fire. The assembled, but as yet untested, machine was exhibited at the Aero Show held at London's Olympia in February 1913 as the Destroyer, although it would appear that its designers referred to it as the 18. Unfortunately, it proved nose heavy and was wrecked during its first attempt to take off. However, the design had promise and work began on a modified version designated as the 18a.

This variant, almost a complete redesign, had no stagger and its undercarriage was incorporated in twin skids. The nacelle had clear panels in the sides, presumably to improve the view downwards, and power was provided by a 100-hp Gnome rotary engine. Testing by company test pilot Harold Barnwell commenced around October 1913.

A further development designated as the model 18b, without the clear panels to the nacelle and fitted with ailerons on all four wings, was at Brooklands in January 1914 and exhibited at Olympia in March. It was later fitted with a triangular fin. Both 18a and 18b were purchased by the War Office, an order also being placed for a further six examples.

A further development of the basic design—with a new nacelle and with the gun mounted above the cockpit rim thereby increasing its field of fire—was designated as the EFB4 (Experimental Fighting Biplane No. 4) with the previous machines now being regarded retrospectively as EFB1-3. The new machine had the same wings as its predecessor with tubular steel struts and a similar undercarriage (with longer skids) and a modified nacelle and tail surfaces. Following testing, it was delivered to the Admiralty in fulfilment of the original order for a fighting biplane early in 1914 and was given the serial number 32 (in accordance with current practice, the Navy's type number for the design). During 1914 and early 1915, it was stationed at RNAS Eastchurch to intercept Zeppelins attacking London, but there is no record of any action. It was transferred to No. 2 Squadron RNAS in March 1915 but was replaced shortly afterwards.

EFB5 differed from previous examples with a further modified nacelle and revised fin. Also, the rudder and struts were of spruce instead of steel employed previously. Power remained the 100-hp Gnome Monosoupape rotary engine. Completed by mid-July 1914, it was flown by Harold Barnwell from Joyce Green near the company works at Crayford to Brooklands on 17 July. EFB5 was then flown to Farnborough a few days later for testing by the AID. On 21 July, it was flown by three RFC pilots, Major H. R. M. Brooke-Popham, Capt. R. Cholmondeley and 2 Lt T. O'B. Hubbard, whose opinions were generally favourable, especially regarding the provision of the machine gun. Col. F. H. Sykes, then commanding the RFC, forwarded their three reports to the Director General of Military Aviation with a recommendation that an order be placed. On 25 July, EFB5 was blown over in a high wind and was returned to the workshops to be repaired.

A further development with unequal span wings, EFB6 had no decking between the two seats. Tested at Brooklands on 14 July, it was decided that the EFB5 should be the version adopted for production, its designation changing to Fighting Biplane No. 5 or FB5. Officially named as the Vickers Fighting Biplane, it was dubbed more affectionately as the Vickers Fighter by those who flew it. The name 'Gunbus' appears to have been invented by the press and applied indiscriminately to any armed pusher.

In response to demands for aeroplanes to expand the flying services, six machines were delivered after the outbreak of the war. This completed the order placed at the end of 1913 and were allocated the serial numbers 649, 664, 682, 686, 704 and 747. These also included the experimental models FB4 and FB6 with the former becoming 664 and the latter 704. None of these machines went to France although the first machine delivered, 664, was taken on charge on 10 September 1914. This particular FB5 saw action on Christmas Day when it was piloted by 2 Lt M. R. Chidson and took off from Joyce Green to intercept an enemy Friedrichshafen floatplane that was following the course of the River Thames. It was chased out to sea where the FB5's gunner, Corporal Martin, fired at it and reported that the enemy aircraft has been damaged.

A few weeks later, another FB5 from Joyce Green, flown by Capt. Robert Maxwell Pike—a former naval officer who had trained as a pilot and joined the RFC despite a limp caused by an injured knee—took off in pursuit of a Zeppelin raider, but engine failure cut the mission short. Force landing in the dark, the FB5 hit a dyke and overturned. The resulting crash caused extensive damage to the FB5 although Pike and his gunner, A. M. Shaw, were unhurt. 647 and 682 were assigned to No. 7 Squadron during October 1914 and by the following January, 649 and 664 had been converted to dual control, the former being assigned

Vickers, EFB4, at RNAS Eastchurch wearing the serial number 32 on its rudder and fitted with a belt-fed Vickers machine gun.

Frank Goodden in the pilot's seat of the first production FB5. The observer's gun is a drum-fed Lewis.

to No. 11 Squadron during February. 747 was transferred to the RNAS at Dover in February, but was struck off charge by the middle of April. It is probable that Vickers put the FB5 into production immediately as the design was finalised before the outbreak of war and the first production example was completed during October 1914. It differed from the prototype in having a straight trailing edge to the rudder so that all surfaces were almost rectangular in shape, presumably to simplify production. Orders were placed both by the Admiralty (861–4) and War Office (2340–7) on 14 August 1914 with the War Office placing three further orders, each for twelve machines, over the next few months. Serials assigned to these were 1616–27, 1628–39 and 1640–51. An enlarged rudder with a curved trailing edge was introduced from serial number 1638. Additional machines were ordered with deliveries being almost continuous and manufacture was also under taken by Darracq S.A. in France.

The first Vickers fighter to go to France, 1621, joined No. 2 Squadron on 5 February 1915 and acted as an escort to its reconnaissance machines where it was flown by 2 Lt Chidson. It then took up a similar role with the newly formed No. 16 Squadron a few days later and more machines joined other squadrons on the same piecemeal basis as soon as they became available. 1621 had a fairly brief operational career as it came down behind enemy lines on 2 March and was captured intact. No. 5 Squadron received at total of nine FB5s between February and June 1915, but only had three on strength by the end of that period. It operated one flight of fighters plus two reconnaissance machines the fighters were intended to protect. However, the Vickers were unable to escort the reconnaissance machines due to a disparity in speed, the Vickers proving slower than their unarmed companions and so patrolled the area ahead of their intended operations. Fredrick Powell, then a newly qualified pilot with No. 5 Squadron, recalled:

This three-quarter rearview of 2343 shows the engine installation and fuel tank. The long tailskid is also noteworthy.

It was an interesting little aeroplane with a Monosoupape engine which had no throttle. You couldn't go fast or slow, it only had one speed: flat out. We used to do two-hour patrols. It had petrol for 2½ hours, so that allowed 15 minutes each way to get to the lines.

The Monosoupape engine was far from reliable with those built under licence by Peter Hooker Ltd proving even worse than those manufactured in France and engine failures were common leading to aborted patrols and forced landings. So bad was the situation that Col. Brooke-Popham, then a staff officer in France, complained to the War Office that one Vickers pilot had suffered twenty-two forced landings due to engine failure in thirty flights and demanded an improvement in engine reliability. However, although such an improvement was eventually achieved, the engine never lived down its reputation for unreliability.

A few of the first machines were fitted with a belt-fed Vickers machine gun instead of the lighter drum-fed Lewis that was quickly standardised. Initial problems with the gun mounting resulted in several changes of design, the Vickers No. 2 Mk 1 eventually being adopted. This, however, was far from perfect and several improved variants were developed by squadron engineers in France. The Lewis guns had the barrel cooling jackets removed, reducing their weight as it was considered that the air flow over the weapon would provide sufficient cooling; however, it was not unknown for the barrel to overheat and gunners restricted themselves to ten-round bursts.

In April, No. 7 Squadron flew to France with two flights of R.E.5 bombers and one of Vickers fighters, including 1637 and 1651, adding to the number patrolling over the lines. Other squadrons operated the type, in addition to their other machines, in a similar role. Lt W. Acland of No. 5 Squadron with A. M. Rogers as his observer shot down an enemy machine on 15 May, their Vickers armed with a rifle as well as a machine gun.

The first squadron fully equipped with the FB5 and the RFC's first ever squadron dedicated solely to aerial fighting was No. 11 that first formed in February 1915. It flew to France on 25 July with eight FB5s in two complete flights, including 1632, 1641, 1643, 1647 and 1650. It received a further three aircraft via the Aircraft Park in a week with the third flight being made up to full strength soon after. By the end of August, the squadron had been issued as replacements with two machines: 5454 and 5455 built by Darracq. The squadron began patrolling its section of the front almost as soon as it arrived in France. Capt. Lionel Rees with Flt Sgt Hargreaves in the front cockpit shot down a Fokker on 17 July despite damage to their own machine.

Vickers FB5, 2878, at Farnborough, its only national marking being the small Union Jack painted on the fin. Its Lewis gun has no ammunition drum fitted.

However, pilots often found that the enemy was disinclined to fight and often being faster than the FB5, simply sped away to avoid combat. This, however, was counted as a success as it freed the skies of enemy machines and allowed the RFC to carry out their duties of reconnaissance, bombing, photography and artillery observation unmolested.

But not all enemy machines refused to fight. On 5 September, another No. 11 Squadron machine flown by 2 Lt Cooper with 2 Lt A. J. Insall as his observer was patrolling near Gommecourt at about 9,000 feet when they spotted an LVG below them. As they dived down in pursuit, the enemy gunner—who occupied the rear cockpit and was equipped with a swivel-mounted machine gun—returned fire. When they grew level, the LVG turned broadside so it could continue to bring its gun to bear. Shots continued to be exchanged in this way until the LVG plunged into a steep dive with black smoke and flames pouring from its exhaust. Indeed, witnesses on the ground confirmed that the LVG was in a steep dive when it ploughed into the ground. Insall later wrote in his account of his part in the war this appreciation of the Vickers FB5 and its noisy rotary engine:

It never pretended to be capable of setting speed or height records. It was quite happy bumbling along above the German Army, booming it its sonorous defiance for all to hear and never evading a trial of strength.

Two days later, a No. 11 Squadron FB5 flown by Capt. Playfair also encountered an LVG; however, it dived away rather than fight. Later the same day, Capt. Darley had a similar experience with an Aviatik, an experience reported several times by other crews over the next few days. Other squadrons had similar experiences although on 29 July, Capt. Reese and Capt. Kennedy from No. 4 Squadron attacked an enemy two-seater that descended into a steep spiral. It returned fire up at the Vickers and hit it in the lower wing damaging both spars, cutting several wires and breaking a rib, although the machine landed successfully.

19 September saw No. 5 Squadron's Lt F. J. Powell together with A. M. Shaw on patrol to the east of Polygon Wood when they observed an LVG below and dived down to attack. The enemy promptly dived away but they spotted a large twin-engine enemy machine and closed to within 100 yards before opening fire, the enemy returning fire from two separate guns. Shaw's aim was true as an engine stopped and the enemy machine dived for the ground while trailing black smoke.

On 31 August, Capt. Lionel Rees with Flt Sgt Hargreaves claimed an Albatros CII. On 21 September, they added an Ago C.I to their score and seven days later spotted an enemy two-seater some 2,000 feet below them, and dived to attack. Their opponent turned out to be both faster and superior than the Vickers having two guns to their one; however, they pressed home their attack and were rewarded by seeing it crash just inside the German frontline. Rees was awarded the Military Cross for this action and other similar examples of courage in the face of superior

Algernon J. Insall adjusting the Lewis gun of a Vickers FB5 prior to take off. The engine is running and a mechanic stands by the wingtip ready to help the machine manoeuvre while taxiing.

forces, and eventually scored a total of seven victories flying the FB5, the highest score of any pilot of the type. Hargreaves was awarded a Distinguished Conduct Medal for his part in the successes.

26 October saw 5459, a No. 5 Squadron machine flown by the famous actor and pioneer airman, Robert Loraine, dive after an Albatros two-seater. He gave chase from 9,000 feet to just 600 feet with the observer, Lt. the Hon. Eric Lubbock, firing at it and Loraine joining in with a pillar-mounted Lewis gun. The enemy pilot, a corporal, was fatally hit and the machine crashed 20 yards from the frontline held by the Canadians. The observer, Lt Buchholz, who was just 17 years old and wounded in the stomach, was taken prisoner and extensively interrogated, a great deal of useful information being obtained. Both Loraine and Lubbock were awarded the Military Cross for the action. Loraine later dropped a message onto the German aerodrome giving details of the crew's fate and returning the pilot's personal effects. Loraine's was not the only Vickers FB5 armed with a second Lewis machine gun. At least one machine of No. 11 Squadron was similarly equipped, although the task of aiming the swivelling gun while flying the aeroplane meant that the chances of hitting a target was virtually nil.

Capt. Rees scored again on 31 October, claiming an LVG two-seater driven down, his observer on this occasion being Flt Sgt Raymond.

On 7 November 1915, 2 Lt Gilbert Insall of No. 11 Squadron was flying 5074 with AM T. H. Donald in the front seat patrolling the Adinfer-Bapaume area when at 2.30 p.m., they spotted an Aviatik some 1,000 feet above them and Insall immediately climbed to attack. The enemy machine began to move away, trying to lead them into range of an anti-aircraft rocket battery. However, Donald's shots found their mark and the Aviatik was shot down and landed heavily in a ploughed field. As the crew struggled away from the machine, Insall returned and dropped an incendiary bomb that left the Aviatik wreathed in smoke. Under fire from the ground, the Vickers headed back and crossed the lines at 2,000 feet where it was hit in several places, including the petrol tank. This caused the engine to stop and Insall managed to land about 500 feet behind the lines in the cover of small wood. Although they were unable to observe the aircraft, German artillery began shelling the area. Around 150 shells were fired, fortunately none further damaging the machine and after nightfall, they managed to repair the machine by the light of screened lamps and took off at dawn where they returned to their aerodrome. Insall was awarded the Victoria Cross for his courage but was unable to be invested with the medal as both he and Donald were shot down and captured a week later. Insall managed to escape on his third attempt in August 1917 and returned to active service with No. 51 Squadron.

During the summer of 1915, the enemy introduced the Fokker monoplane fighter armed with a forward firing machine gun. This innovative design changed the nature of aerial combat overnight; however, the Fokker, along with other similar designs, was initially available in very small numbers. Despite the FB5's obsolescence, the type was obliged to continue in service, to counter the new oppositions as best it could, and on 19 November, the number operating in France increased by the arrival of No. 18 Squadron that was equipped with it. Losses increased and victories became ever more elusive, especially as most enemy machines were faster than the FB5. When during November 1915, a No. 11 Squadron machine courageously attempted to engage a Fokker, the enemy simply sped away in a steep dive.

On 16 March 1916, over a year since the type first entered service in France, Trenchard wrote to the Deputy Director of Military Aeronautics to state that 'The Vickers Fighters, in their present condition, are now hopelessly outclassed and must be considered as quite out of date.' Trenchard's wish was granted and the type was withdrawn from active

Gilbert Martin Insall whose courageous recovery in 5074 earned him a Victoria Cross.

service from the spring of 1916. A number of machines were reassigned to training units in the UK. No. 18 Squadron exchanged its FB5s for the Royal Aircraft Factory F.E.2b, although No. 11 Squadron soldiered on with their Vickers until July.

The type had made a big impact and lived on in spirit after its withdrawal from the Western Front. When Manfred von Richthofen (The Red Baron) achieved his first victory on 17 September, he claimed that he had shot down an F.E.2b when it was a FB5. Twelve were built under licence in Denmark and were completed around March 1916. Although they saw no action, the Danish FB5s remained in service until 1924, the last of the design to survive.

In an attempt to improve the performance of the fighter, a modified design, the FB9, appeared in late 1915. Slightly smaller than the FB5 with a wingspan of just under 34 feet, it had rounded tips to the wings and tailplane, and was braced by streamlined Rafwires. Like the previous variant, power was provided by the 100-hp Gnome Monosoupape. The nose contour of the nacelle was more streamlined, giving an improved appearance as did the vee undercarriage, similar to that which had replaced the twin-skid version on some later production FB5s. Prototype 7665 was tested by the Central Flying School on 5 January 1916 and was sent to No. 11 Squadron in France for evaluation by service crews the following day. Opinions by pilots were generally favourable although observers were somewhat critical of the reduced leg room afforded by the revised nose contours and of the gun mounting.

7665 appears to have remained with No. 11 Squadron for on 2 April, it was flown by Capt. Champion de Crespigny with 2 Lt J. Hughes-Chamberlain as his observer and attacked a group of five enemy aircraft. One was shot down and a second dived out of control before the FB5 was shot up so badly with the rudder controls inoperative, it crash landed and was struck off charge. A total of ninety-five FB5s were built by Vickers with a further twenty-four built by Darracq, several of which found their way to No. 11 Squadron, the first, 7812, arriving on 19 May. One of these, 7828, scored a combat victory on 1 July 1916 while flown by Lt Moyes and Sgt Glover.

Like the FB5, the FB9 was withdrawn from frontline service by the end of July. Many finished their careers with training units where some were provided with dual controls, the nacelle noses being modified to improve leg room.

German soldiers examine a shot down Vickers FB5. The missing fabric allows the construction to be seen.

The more streamlined FB9 served mostly at training units. This one, A1429, being with the School of Aerial Gunnery at Hythe.

AIRCO DH1

The Aircraft Manufacturing Company, later known as Airco, was founded in 1912 by the entrepreneur George Holt Thomas. Based in Hendon, the company principally manufactured French designs, mostly Farman aircraft under licence. In the spring of 1914, they were joined by Geoffrey de Havilland—as both chief designer and test pilot—who recruiting design staff and started work on a new fighter. De Havilland's original thoughts, in order to obtain the best possible performance, were for a tractor type. However, the War Office was of the opinion that the observer's field of fire was the most important consideration in a fighting aircraft and Thomas insisted that the new machine must be a pusher. De Havilland therefore tried to achieve the cleanest design and the best performance possible, but before the project could be completed, war broke out and de Havilland, a lieutenant in the RFC Reserve, was called up for active service. He initially joined No. 2 Squadron at Farnborough, but a medical board found him unfit for duty overseas as he was recovering from the injuries he had sustained in a S.E.2 crash the previous year. Therefore, de Havilland was posted to Montrose in Scotland to fly anti-submarine patrols in an unarmed Blériot monoplane. Common sense prevailed and before the month was out, he had been recalled to Farnborough to serve as a test pilot, effectively the same job he had before joining Airco. Meanwhile, Thomas campaigned for his release and after some three months of hard bargaining, de Havilland returned to the drawing office at Hendon. At the time, de Havilland was still a serving officer and obliged to wear a uniform. Also, he was subject to an instant recall to service.

Before the end of 1914 with the DH1 (as the new machine was designated) nearing completion, the project received another setback. It had been designed to be powered by a 100-hp six-cylinder Green engine, but the limited production of these units was reserved for the Royal Aircraft Factory's F.E.2a. As the first batch was nearing completion, the best available alternative was a V8 Renault rated at just 70 hp. Completed early in the New Year, the prototype was designed to have a small stub wing projecting from either side of the nacelle that could be turned at right angles to the airflow to act as air brakes, preventing any float when landing, and allowing the machine to land in small fields. Unusually, the vee undercarriage included coil springs with small oleo dampers to absorb landing shocks, but the machine was otherwise fairly conventional. Its un-staggered wings employed two bay bracing, the central portion of the wings—as far outboard as the first pair of struts being rigged flat with the outer portions rigged with a few degrees of dihedral—to give lateral stability. The rudder was carried on tubular tail booms with the tailplane and elevators mounted on top of the upper pair, surmounted by a low-aspect-ratio fin. Initially, the forward cockpit had high sides offering the occupant protection from the elements, but such protection limited the use of a weapon and these were later modified. Armament, when fitted, was a pillar-mounted Lewis gun on the nose of the nacelle with the clear field of fire considered of paramount importance. The mounting was designed by de Havilland and subject to a patent taken out on 7 June 1915.

Flight testing was sufficiently advanced by 30 January for de Havilland to fly two circuits of Hendon Aerodrome with his hands held above his head, steering only with the rudder, in order to demonstrate the machine's stability. This very public trial was reported, along with a fairly detailed description of the design and a number of photographs, in the aeronautical press. Performance figures, which might have been of practical use to the enemy, were not given although *Flight* commented that the machine looked fast. If so, appearances were deceptive as it could manage just 78 mph, a creditable performance given the low power of the engine, but far from an advance in aeroplane design. Climb was equally leisurely at less than 500 feet per minute.

When de Havilland flew the DH1 to Farnborough on 4 February for its official appraisal, the air brakes, which provided no actual benefit, had been removed and the serial 4220 applied. The DH1's merits were obvious for it was faster than the Vickers FB5 and cheaper to build than the F.E.2a, both of which were in production and an order for a further forty-nine units was placed. This gave the Aircraft Manufacturing Company something of a problem as they were working to a full capacity on the construction of Farman trainers and the order was subcontracted to Savages of Kings Lynn, then famous as builders of fairground equipment. Although Savages' workshops possessed all the skills and equipment necessary for the manufacture of aeroplanes, this was the company's first such venture and it was not until 7 November that the first production DH1, 4600, was delivered to Farnborough for handing over to the RFC. It and other production examples differed from the prototype in that the coil springs had been discarded. The axle was bound to the apexes of the undercarriage vees with rubber shock cord in the then conventional manner.

By this time, the introduction of the Fokker and similar fighters had changed the nature of aerial warfare. The two-seat pusher was helplessly outclassed and no DH1s were sent to France. Instead, they found a new role in training and home defence units in the UK. Although production DH1s were fitted with a Renault engine uprated

The prototype DH1 at Hendon where it was built. The stub wings intended for use as air brakes can be seen on the side of the nacelle behind the cockpit. The high sides of the front cockpit would have prevented a gun being fitted.

The prototype DH1 without its airbrakes fitted, the hole for their operating shaft is just visible to the rear of the forward-centre section strut.

An early production example of DH1A, 4606, with the observer's windscreen in place. No gun is fitted although the cockpit sides are now lower.

to 80 hp, an improvement was obtained by increasing the cylinder bore by 5 mm; however, its performance remained unspectacular. In an effort to bring about a radical enhancement, a number of designated DH1As were fitted with the six-cylinder inline water-cooled Beardmore engine developing 120 hp. This engine also powered the Royal Aircraft Factory's hugely successful F.E.2b and on 5 June 1916, DH1A, 4605, was flown at the Central Flying School in a direct comparison with F.E.2b, 6337. Not surprisingly, the de Havilland design, being both smaller and lighter, proved superior in speed, rate of climb, and manoeuvrability. The test report stated that 'both machines are stable and easy to fly, but the de Havilland is quicker to manoeuvre and lighter on the controls'. However, the F.E.2b, which was already in large-scale production, enjoyed a longer range. Also, in the bombing role where its future ultimately lay, it could carry a far greater load, so production of the DH1A was limited to the completion of those already on order.

Like the lower-powered DH1, the F.E.2b served mostly with home defence and training units, but in July 1916, six were shipped to the Middle East. Four units, 4607–10, joined No. 14 Squadron that operated in both Egypt and Palestine as fighter/reconnaissance machines. On 23-25 July, these DH1As, acting as escorts to B.E.2c reconnaissance machines, engaged enemy aircraft, but the combats were inconclusive with one observer slightly wounded during an engagement and 4607 damaged in another. On 2 August 1916, 4609, crewed by Lts McLaren and West, scored what appears to have been the type's only combat victory. After firing two drums of ammunition at fairly close range, it shot down an Aviatik two-seater that forced landed near Bir Salmana. However, 4608 was shot down on 5 March 1917 while acting as an escort during a bombing raid on Tel el Sheria. The fighter crashed near to Tel el Jemmi and its crew taken prisoner. 4610 was struck of charge on 23 August and the remaining two machines survived until 1 November when they were struck off charge, ending the type's active service career.

Back in the UK, the DH1, like most unwanted aeroplanes, served with a number of training units. No. 9 Reserve Squadron at Norwich had at least three, including 4619 and 4626, on strength and in a cruel twist of fate the type provided a useful intermediate trainer for pilots destined for F.E.2bs.

Close-up of the nacelle of a DH1A with No. 14 Squadron in the Middle East showing the water-cooled Beardmore engine that distinguished it from earlier variants. Note the skull and crossbones marking on the nose.

DH1, A1635, with No. 17 Reserve Squadron at Port Meadow in Oxfordshire.

A total of 100 DH1/1As were manufactured and all subcontracted to Savages while at least three more, A5211, A9919 and B3969, were reconstructed from spares at the depot.

ROYAL AIRCRAFT FACTORY B.E.9

In the spring of 1915 with dogfighting in its infancy, staff of the Royal Aircraft Factory created an innovative but bizarre attempt to combine the field of fire only available in a pusher with the aerodynamic advantages of a tractor in one machine: the B.E.9. Possibly inspired by a similar design patented by the French company SPAD in February 1915, this new machine had the passenger placed in a small nacelle mounted forwards of the propeller of a tractor design. This was based on what was then the most effective general purpose aeroplane available, the Factory's B.E.2c, which had evolved from a design by de Havilland as a benchmark against which competitors in the 1912 Military Aeroplane Competition could be judged. It proved generally superior to almost every competitor and was ordered into production, becoming the mainstay of the RFC at the beginning of the war. Drawings for the B.E.9 were completed by June 1915 and then, rather than build an aeroplane from scratch, the Factory team took a standard production example, 1700, built by the British and Colonial Aeroplane Company, which was delivered to Farnborough on 21 June 1915. This was an early model and powered by a 70-hp Renault engine that was removed and returned to the stores for reissue. The fuselage was shortened and the engine—a 90-hp RAF1a as fitted to the latest model B.E.2c—was moved back into the space previously occupied by the forward cockpit, bringing the propeller closer to the upper wing. The centre-section struts were splayed outwards to clear the cylinders of the V8 engine, widening the centre section and adding about 4 feet to the wingspan. The lower wings were similarly extended, but with a small gap retained at the root so as to improve the downward view from the pilot's cockpit. The original tailplane, elevators and rudder were retained, but a greatly enlarged fin was fitted to offset the effect of the increase in keel area forwards of the centre of gravity. A taller air scoop was provided in an attempt to ensure sufficient air flow to keep the engine cool.

The observer was provided with a plywood nacelle mounted via a ball race on a forward extension of the propeller shaft supported by four additional struts added to the undercarriage and secured by bracing wires to the wings. Two alternative shapes had been designed for the nacelle—a faired design that was almost ovoid and a simpler variant whose sides blended to the fuselage contours. Models of both were subjected to wind tunnel tests which established that the latter was the more efficient and this was adopted for manufacture. A metal hoop on the rear rim of the nacelle served to remind the occupant of the propeller revolving immediately behind.

The modified machine was submitted for final inspection on 13 August, approval being given early the following afternoon and Frank Goodden took it up for a brief test flight at 5.45 p.m. the same day. The Factory was preparing for a visit by King George V and Queen Mary on 18 August and test flying appears to have been suspended until this was over. However, the B.E.9 was one of the machines exhibited for their royal inspection and it attracted a great deal of interest. The day after, test flying resumed with both Goodden and William Stutt making frequent flights in the B.E.9, many of them with staff members experiencing the forward cockpit.

Work had already begun on the design of a more powerful version, the B.E.9a, with a 140-hp V12 RAF4a engine that was being developed. By 20 August, a crude sketch of this proposal had reached Col. H. R. M. Brooke-Popham who circulated copies to squadron commanders, along with the following request:

The B.E.9 at Farnborough. The varnished plywood of the observer's nacelle contrasts strongly with the doped fabric covering. Although the observer's field of fire is superb, his loneliness is easy to imagine.

King George V made several visits to the Royal Aircraft Factory. Here he is being shown the B.E.9 on 18 August 1915.

Please give your opinion of the proposed type of aeroplane. The question should be considered from the point of view of the observer as well as that of general utility.

Responses were returned with commendable speed, none taking longer than a day or two. Some reports were brief as Brooke-Popham's own handwritten note, other typed reports extended over several pages. Almost all commented favourably on the field of fire afforded by the observer's position. However, adverse comments were made on the lack of communication between pilot and observer, engine cooling and the possible loss of propeller efficiency. The vulnerability of the observer was also noted by the CO of No. 1 Squadron commenting that:

The supply of good observers is small and will be further reduced if machines of this type do even moderately bad landings in the small landing grounds that the RFC's squadron now occupy.

An officer from No. 1 Wing added that he had sat in the prototype while on a visit to Farnborough and suggested that the machine should be given 'a good trial', whereas No. III Wing was of the opinion that 'the Royal Aircraft Factory should be instructed to design an improved machine of the pusher type', presumably unaware that with the introduction of the F.E.2b this had already been done. The reports were forwarded to headquarters on 24 August but had no effect on the progress of the B.E.9's development. The type had acquired its most obvious nickname, the Pulpit, and was more often referred to the title Pulpit B.E.2 than by its official designation.

On 25 August 1915, 1700 was flown to Netheravon for assessment by the Central Flying School, remaining there until 31 August. On this date, a report signed by Capt. Godfrey Paine RN was issued, describing the design as 'excellent' with a field of fire 'better than any seen here'. The top speed was measured at 82 mph with climb to 4,000 feet taking 12 minutes and 40 seconds. Stability was judged to be 'very good', although the provision of a tailplane trimmer was recommended. Other recommendations were the provision of dual controls, at least on the rudder and elevators, and efficient telephonic communication between the crew as the device that was currently fitted was considered as 'No use.' A handwritten note, on the copy of the report retained in the National Archive, states confidently that 'we can get over most of these difficulties' and the Factory made an effort to do so. Dual control, comprising a control stick for the elevators together with hand grips to operate the rudder, was provided on extensions to the control cables, which followed a rather torturous route via the undercarriage struts. No improved communication for the crew could be provided and the request for a tail trimmer was also ignored.

After taking part in trials connected with the development of improved air speed indicators, 1700 was flown to the depot at St Omer on 11 September 1915 and piloted by Flt Cdr C. D. Breeze, RNAS.

Col. Brooke-Popham lost little time in trying it out for himself and by 14 September, had prepared a report in which he described a ride in the passenger seat. He noted that the rate of climb was 25 minutes to reach 6,000 feet and the view was 'excellent'. Brooke-Popham compared the experience as if flying a Henri Farman and he found the presence of the propeller behind him as 'not in the least disconcerting'. He confirmed that crew communication was an issue but was confident that the Royal Aircraft Factory was working towards a solution. Also, even though the forward cockpit was 'quite comfortable', even in a steep dive, he did suggest that a cap be fitted over the end of the propeller shaft where it entered the rear of the nacelle.

Engine overheating proved a problem on longer flights and the cylinders had to be replaced at the depot. On 18 September, it was flown to No. 6 Squadron based at Abeele by Capt. L. G. Hawker VC. Despite

Head-on view of a B.E.9 showing the gaps at the lower wing roots which allowed the pilot a downward view.

continuous engine problems, the B.E.9 made several test flights with the squadron and flew at least one patrol over the lines. The squadron's personnel found it easy to fly and land, but criticised the separation of the crew for which they found the speaking tube then fitted to be 'no compensation'. After further work on the overheating engine, it was moved on 21 September to No. 16 Squadron. The commanding officer, Major H. C. T. Dowding, wrote a lengthy report confirming that the climb was slow when compared to the B.E.2c with which his squadron was then equipped, and that the passenger's view was excellent. Also, it was so stable in flight that the pilot could let go of the controls and shoot to the rear to defend against attackers if provided with a gun. However, Dowding also commented that he considered it to be dangerous for the passenger if the B.E.9 should nose over 'as the B.E. often does in soft ground'.

It was returned to the depot after a few days and tested by No. 2 Squadron and was then passed on to No. 8 Squadron based at Marieux where it was flown, among others, by Capt. W. S. Douglas who took it up twice on 8 October. A. M. Smith on his first flight in the front seat lasted just 10 minutes and his second, with A. M. Clayton, for 20 minutes, during which time he took it up to 3,000 feet. Douglas recorded in his logbook that he found the B.E.9 to be 'rather sluggish, but very stable'.

On 13 October, Lt Glen, during a patrol over the lines, had a brief but inconclusive encounter with an enemy aircraft. His combat report

The B.E.9 in flight. Service markings have been applied and the observer's nacelle is occupied. Although, as no gun is fitted to the mounting, the location is most likely to be somewhere in the UK.

aroused far more interest in the type of armament fitted to his opponent that had circled around him than the performance of the B.E.9. This was perhaps due to further evaluate the performance of the Fokker, which although had been in action for several months, was an uncommon sight.

At least one other pilot took the B.E.9 over the lines. On 26 October, Capt. Douglas flew it on a reconnaissance patrol lasting for over an hour, his observer being A. M. Walker, reputedly the best gunner in the squadron. Douglas noted that the enemy anti-aircraft gunners held their fire, possibly because they were unsure of the identity of 'this strange apparition'. He also commented that although several enemy aircraft were seen, 1700 was too slow to catch them and Walker was therefore unable to test his skill as a gunner.

The cooling of the RAF1a engine, which was marginal at the best of times—the type usually ran on an over-rich mixture to help keep cylinder head temperatures down—proved too great a problem to overcome in the B.E.9. In just under 48 hours flying time, 1700 was fitted with three replacement engines, one of which seized after 85 minutes in addition to fourteen new cylinders and other modifications. Despite the undoubted excellence of its forward view and field of fire, the B.E.9's performance was sluggish, especially when turning and the problem of crew communication remained unresolved. It is no surprise that at the end of its extensive service trials in France, Brig-Gen. Trenchard concluded that 'this type of aeroplane cannot be recommended'.

An exchange of correspondence between the Deputy Assistant Quartermaster General in France and the Assistant Director of Military Aeronautics at the War Office established that it was not to be dismantled for spares, but should be returned to the Royal Aircraft Factory. 1700 was therefore returned to the depot at St Omer by Capt. Douglas where it remained until 9 January 1916 when Sgt Maj. Power flew it to Farnborough, its last recorded flight.

The more powerful B.E.9a was never built.

AIRCO DH2

Almost as soon as his work on the DH1 was complete, Geoffrey de Havilland began on a scaled down, single-seat version of the same basic design, the DH2, which was to be powered by a 100-hp Gnome rotary engine. The prototype was completed by the end of May 1915 and fitted with a Lewis gun on the portside of the nacelle. Its mounting, which was similar to that of the DH1, was covered with an aluminium fairing as an aid to streamlining. Its first flight, piloted by de Havilland, was made on 1 June and although cut short due to a misfiring engine, it revealed that the little pusher was tail heavy. Flown again the next day with 30 lb of ballast in the nose as a temporary solution to the balance problem, it climbed to 3,000 feet in five minutes. However, de Havilland thought that the fin and rudder were too small, an issue he had encountered before in scaled down designs and which had been partially responsible for the crash of the S.E.2 in 1913.

It was therefore returned to the workshops where the nacelle was moved forwards four inches and the tail structure rebuilt while a larger rudder, including a small balance area forward of the pivot point, replaced the original surface. Two weeks later, it was back in the air, its balance problems resolved and speed measured at a maximum of 93 mph.

Capt. R. M. Pike, then a Vickers fighter pilot with No. 5 Squadron, was sent to Hendon to inspect and test the DH2, which he was able to do on 22 June after de Havilland completed some test flying of his own. Pike was generally enthusiastic about the little pusher reporting that 'she will be of tremendous value', but was critical of the way in which the instrument board vibrated and also recommended that wing-tip skids were fitted, along with drift wires from the nacelle to the wings. These modifications and others suggested by de Havilland were completed and the serial 4732 applied before it was sent to France for service trials joining No. 5 Squadron at Abeele on 26 July 1915. Two days later, while flown by Pike, it took part in a tentative engagement with a large Aviatik about which he submitted this report:

> I saw a German machine about three miles away and rapidly overhauled him. He had no idea of the speed of my machine and attempted to evade me by climbing. I caught him up and fired a drum at him from about 100 to 80 yards. I then turned to reload and found that the clip on the drum had stuck. I lost sight of the German while struggling with the drum, but heard his machine gun going until the belt had finished.

On 9 August, Pike engaged two German aeroplanes near Zonnebeke, sending one down before suffering a head wound that brought him down behind enemy lines. Pike died almost immediately and 4732 fell into enemy hands. RFC HQ was not informed of its loss until two days later after a message had been dropped near St Omer by Theo Osterkamp containing details of Pike's burial with full military honours. The Germans were keen to evaluate this new opponent and repaired the damage to 4732 caused by its forced landing, during which

Geoffrey de Havilland uses a step ladder to study the prototype DH2 at Hendon in June 1915. The machine has the original small tail surfaces. (*L. Everett*)

The prototype DH2 at Hendon. The front of the nacelle has a slot to allow a machine gun to be elevated.

it had overturned, including constructing a new rudder so it could be flown. The loss of the prototype DH2 was a serious setback, but the design had made a sufficiently good impression for production orders to be placed with the Aeroplane Manufacturing Company, construction being undertaken at Hendon. Production examples differed from the prototype by having their machine gun mounted immediately in front of the pilot with a small windscreen attached directly to it although the gun was still arranged to swivel.

The first production machine, 5916, was completed during November 1915 and was vigorously tested. The second and third machines, 5917 and 5918, were initially intended to go to France, but on 28 November, sent to the Central Flying School. One was flown in comparison tests with the F.E.8, although no report of the results has survived.

In accordance with current practice, the next few machines were attached as escorts to squadrons operating other types. The first was issued to No. 5 Squadron that was equipped with the Vickers FB5 powered by the 100-hp Gnome engine and flown regularly by Lt Frederick and J. Powell. 5619 went to another Vickers squadron, No. 18, at Treizennes on 8 January 1916. It was joined the following day by 5620 that was ferried from England by Capt. Hereward de Havilland, the designer's brother, who flew the squadron's first patrol two days later. Testing completed, 5616 joined the squadron and on 5 February, scored the type's first victory when Capt. Cunningham engaged an Albatros two-seater, his bullets damaging the engine and propeller. The enemy made a forced landing as a result.

The DH2 was not popular at first. Pilots who were unused to such a small and high-powered machine found it to be tricky to fly and prone to spinning, a manoeuvre that was then far from perfectly understood and a number of accidents occurred before pilots became fully familiar with the type's flying characteristics. The engine, as was common with rotaries, had no throttle and was provided with a blip switch that cut the ignition. This effectively slowed the engine as an aid to manoeuvring and its use produced a very marked torque reaction as power was suddenly cut or restored. Such an action rocked the machine quite noticeably and pilots found this to be disconcerting until they became used to it.

No. 24 Squadron, which had formed in Hounslow in September 1915, was the first unit to be equipped with the DH2 and became the first single-seat fighter squadron in the RFC. On 7 February, the squadron flew to France and was led by Major L. G. Hawker VC. The journey was not without incident as one pilot who shared their airfield recalled 'Two of 24's pilots had crashed in England on the way and a third, going up for a test flight on the afternoon of their arrival, spun from 300 feet

An unidentified DH2 with a training unit at Hounslow in early 1916.

5943 at Hendon, presumably immediately after completion.

and was killed.' However, once settled in to its new home and role, the squadron began patrolling over enemy-held territory and provided a defensive shield that finally brought an end to the Fokker supremacy as the DH2 was faster and more manoeuvrable. Hawker devised a clamp for the gun, fixing it to fire straight ahead, which incorporated a spring clip so that it could be released to swivel. Although the clamp was adopted for all service machines, the spring clip was seldom employed, pilots enjoying the advantages of having only to fly the aeroplane to aim the gun.

Hawker also put an end to his fear over the DH2's tendency to spin by taking one up to 8,000 feet and deliberately spinning it, both left and right, and recovered perfectly each time. On landing, he explained what he had done and confidence in the little pusher began to grow.

No. 24 Squadron experienced its first combat on 19 March in an inconclusive encounter and achieved its first combat victory on 2 April when 2 Lt D. M. Tidmarsh and Lt Sibley shared the credit for an Albatros two-seater. On 21 April, Tidmarsh suffered a direct hit from an anti-aircraft shell that passed through the nacelle of his DH2, 5924, and in front of his knees without exploding, causing no significant damage except for the large holes made by its passing. Tidmarsh was unaffected by this narrow escape as on 30 April, he spotted a Fokker some 4,000 feet below him and dived to attack only to see it crash into a house at Bapaume without a shot being fired.

5171 was flown in comparison with a Nieuport piloted by Capt. Bell-Irving on 16 April, climbing to 10,000 feet in just under 21 minutes whereas the Nieuport reached the same height in less than twelve minutes. On 17 May, Lt D. Wilson of No. 24 Squadron flew 5989 to Vilacoubley where a similar comparison was carried out against a Nieuport flown by a French pilot, the results being similar, but for manoeuvrability the pusher could easily hold its own. 5925, which joined No. 24 Squadron in March 1916, had a fairly distinguished career bringing down a number of enemy aircraft commencing with a Fokker monoplane that was shot down by Lt S. E. Cowan on 24 April. Several other pilots claimed victories flying 5926 and on 3 November, Lt E. C. Pashley shot down a Halberstadt DII. Later fitted with the propeller from an F.E.8, it remained in action until the spring of 1917, achieving at least three further combat successes before it was returned to the UK on 2 May as unfit for further service.

No. 29 Squadron, which had been raised as a reserve squadron before being reclassified as a fighter unit, received its full complement of twenty DH2s by the end of January 1916 and completed the process of familiarisation as soon as possible. On 24 March, the squadron moved

2 Lt Tidmarsh standing by 5929, its nacelle showing clear evidence of the passage of a shell through it. The step ladder was essential in order to get into the cockpit.

to Dover and flew to France the following day where it landed at St
Omer and its home aerodrome at Abeele on 15 April. Losses due to
unservicability and training accidents meant that the squadron received
a number of replacement aircraft and the journey to France took
a further toll with several forced landings. By the time the squadron
moved to Abeele, it had twelve aircraft fully operational; however, it
took a total of twenty-seven DH2s for this to be achieved. Once in
operation, its pilots began bringing down enemy aircraft and on 1 May,
Lt Segrave shot down a two-seater he described as an Aviatik after firing
just several rounds. DH2 pilots did not have everything their own way.
For example, Capt. E. W. Parrett engaged two enemy aircraft on 29 May
without success, receiving a bullet wound in the head for his trouble,
and force landed near St Eloi. Also, Capt. Clarke was wounded in an
encounter with an enemy aircraft on 8 June. James McCudden who
joined the squadron in July and went on to become one of England's
greatest fighter pilots with fifty-six victories, claimed his first victory on
6 September flying the DH2. McCudden recalled 'The DH2 was a very
cold machine as the pilot had to sit in a small nacelle with the engine a
long way back and so, of course, he got no heat from it at all.' Major
Hawker clearly shared this opinion as he is generally credited with the
invention of 'fug boots' that had the appearance of sheepskin-lined
waders and kept the pilot warm from his feet to mid-thigh.

No. 32 Squadron, the third to be fully equipped with the DH2,
arrived in France on 29 May, further adding to the growing fighter
screen. This helped the RFC take command of the skies over the Western
Front, albeit temporarily, and allowed its squadrons to carry out their
co-operation duties in preparation for the Battle of the Somme, the
huge push forwards that would test the new volunteer army to the full.
The squadron, under the command of Major Lionel Rees MC, began
operations from St Auchel on 6 June, moving to Treizzennes on 7
July so as to be closer to the site of the planned offensive. There was
a great deal of aerial activity in the weeks leading up to the battle and
on 17 June, Capt. Wilkinson of No. 24 Squadron saw a group of six
German aircraft near Arras, the formation breaking up as he attacked.
Two DH2s joined the combat and Wilkinson managed to bring one of
the enemy machines down. On his way back to base, he spotted an
Albatros two-seater that he shot down and then attacked another
hostile machine with his last drum of ammunition. With its propeller
stopped, the enemy went down in a steep dive and appeared to land
without further damage. On the next day, Wilkinson claimed two
further victories, although Lt Nixon of No. 32 Squadron was wounded
in an engagement with five enemy machines.

In training units, it was common for DH2s to have their serial painted on the nacelle as well as the rudder.

On the first day of the Somme offensive on 1 July 1916, Major Rees, the CO of No. 32 Squadron, took off just before 06.00 hours in 6015. Rees observed a formation of a dozen aircraft that he assumed to be British bombers and as he moved closer, he was fired at. Realising his mistake, Rees promptly attacked and one of the enemy machines dived away. Rees fired about thirty rounds at a Roland that fell away in a dive, then continued his attack upon the remaining five or more enemy aircraft, all of which returned fire, a bullet hitting Rees in the thigh. The shock of the wound made Rees giddy and he broke off for a moment, but as soon as his head cleared he returned to the attack, firing until his ammunition was exhausted. He returned to his aerodrome without difficulty and managed to climb out of his cockpit once a ladder was located. Laying on the ground, Rees made his report before having his wound treated, his actions earning him a Victoria Cross. After he recovered, he took command of the School of Aerial Fighting at Ayr.

The introduction of new German fighters such as the Albatros DII and Halberstadt during the autumn of 1916 had returned the advantage to the enemy. With no replacement designs available, the

Major Lionel Rees was
awarded the Victoria Cross
for his actions on 1 July
1916 while flying 6015.

DH2 had to soldier on. Hptm Oswald Boelcke, commander of Jasta 2, scored the DII's first victory on 2 September when he shot down a No. 32 Squadron DH2 piloted by Capt. R. E. Wilson. Boelcke took Wilson on a tour of his unit's base before sending him off to prisoner of war camp.

During the summer of 1916, it was decided that squadron commanders should not fly regular patrols, an instruction that Major L. G. Hawker VC, CO of No. 24 Squadron, amongst others, chose to ignore. At 13.00 hours on 23 November, he took off from Bertangles Aerodrome in 5964, flying as part of 'A' Flight led by Capt. J. O. Andrews along with Capt. R. H. Saundby and Lt J. H. Crutel. At about 13.30 hours, Crutel experienced engine problems and turned back and at 13.50, the remaining three machines attacked two enemy aircraft below them. As they swooped down, Andrews spotted a larger group of enemy fighters above and would have disengaged, but Hawker, with typical aggression, was pressing home his attack. In the ensuing melee, Hawker lost sight of his companions and got involved in a one on one fight with a red Albatros DII flown by Manfred von Richthofen of Jasta 2. After a long battle, during which neither pilot could gain an advantage over his opponent with the Albatros firing almost 900 rounds without effect, Hawker grew low on fuel and broke off to make a dash for the lines. However, a bullet from Richthofen's final burst hit him in the back of the head, killing him instantly and his machine spun to the ground, crashing south of Bapaume. The gun from Hawker's DH2 was salvaged and kept by Richthofen as a trophy, Hawker being his eleventh confirmed victory. Richthofen's next two victims were DH2s with 5986 of No. 32 Squadron, flown by Lt L. P. Hunt being shot down on 11 December near Arras, and 7927 on 20 December. Hunt survived to become a prisoner of war but Capt. Arthur Knight of No. 29 Squadron, the pilot of 7927, was killed. Oswald Boelcke also shot down several DH2s, including No. 24 Squadron's A2542 on 16 October 1916.

A total of 400 DH2s were built by the Aircraft Manufacturing Company at Hendon and of these, 206 went to France, mainly to keep three squadrons up to strength, such was the level of wastage experienced. The DH2 was finally withdrawn from service on the Western Front in June 1917 when Nos 24 and 32 Squadrons changed over to the DH5.

One DH2, A5058, was on strength with the experimental station at Orfordness and on the night of 16/17 June 1917, played a part in the destruction of Zeppelin *L48*. All suitable aeroplanes such as a B.E.2c and an F.E.2b, both equipped for flying at night, took off and Capt. R. H. Saundby was granted permission to join them flying the DH2. His report of the action was:

Oswald Boelcke seated in a downed No. 24 Squadron DH2 while Ltn Otto Hohne and Manfred von Richthofen (in the short coat) look on.

...saw one HA [Hostile Aeroplane] over Harwich going E. at 3.10 a.m. Followed him and climbed up under his tail firing three drums of Pomeroy and tracer at rapidly shortening range. The HA was at this time losing height and I was climbing. I am unable to be certain at what height the engagement took place as I had no dashboard lights and could not read the altimeter. I saw another machine higher than myself and NW of the HA firing bursts of tracer bullets. In the middle of my third drum the HA caught fire at one point and almost immediately became a mass of flame.

Saundby, along with the two pilots with whom he shared credit for the victory, was awarded the Military Cross and thereafter higher-performance machines were allowed to fly at night.

The DH2 also served in the Middle East and remained in active service until the late autumn of 1917. No. 14 Squadron's mixture of aeroplanes included a number of DH2s that served with the DH1 and Bristol Scouts in 'A' Flight, which was later detached and formed into No. 111 Squadron. A4779—which was delivered as was common practice in a packing case together with a spare engine in July 1917—was test flown by Capt. F. W. Stent, commander of the detached special duties flight, on 18 July. A4779 enjoyed a brief but unremarkable career in support of the Arab revolt in the Hejaz region.

One example, 8725, was ordered by the Admiralty but was transferred to the RFC without seeing service with the Navy. Another, A2369, was flying at the Royal Aircraft Factory in Farnborough as late as March 1918 when it took part in experiments with modified controls.

The majority of the remainder served with training units, mostly in the UK, where they often had their serial numbers painted in large characters on the side of the nacelle. James McCudden, who in May 1917 was resting between tours of duty in France as an instructor at Joyce Green, adopted a DH2 for his own use and recalled in his autobiography:

I spun regularly to the great consternation of the pupils there who regarded the machine as a super death trap, not knowing that in its day it was one of the best machines in the RFC.

A fine tribute from Britain's most decorated fighter pilot.

A fine study of 7851 showing the complex rigging including the aileron balance cable running across the upper wing.

ROYAL AIRCRAFT FACTORY F.E.8

The Royal Aircraft Factory applied its talents to the design of a single-seat fighter as soon as the need for such a machine became clear with John Kenworthy completing his design for Fighting Experimental No. 8 or F.E.8 in May 1915. Like rival designers and limited by firing a machine gun past a tractor propeller, Kenworthy's design was a pusher powered by a 100-hp Gnome rotary engine driving a four-blade propeller; however, it introduced a number of innovative features. The nacelle frame was of triangulated steel tube that once constructed required no 'truing up' in service and was covered with shaped panels of aluminium (these covering items required regular inspection as they were secured by laces as was common for fabric.) The oil and petrol tanks were shaped to match the contours of the upper decking and the underside of the nacelle was fitted with light armour to provide protection against ground fire. The tail surfaces had wooden spars and ribs of aluminium alloy punched out to shape with steel fittings and framework. The tail booms did not meet at the rudder post as in other designs, but at the tailplane spar forming a triangle when viewed from the side. Tailplane incidence could be adjusted while the machine was on the ground by moving the retaining bolts around a quadrant and the skid was fastened to the bottom of the rudder post. The wing structure was more conventional, the high-aspect-ratio wings being rigged in two bays and having a generous five degrees of dihedral outboard of the first interplane struts. The ailerons had no balance cables, being returned to their normal position by rubber bungees.

The F.E.8 was designed to be armed with a Lewis gun mounted in the nose of the nacelle, the breech level with the pilot's knees and aimed by means of a small sighting bar mounted above the cockpit rim. Instrumentation was typical for the period and comprised of a compass and clinometer with a direct-drive tachometer, fuel pressure gauge and altimeter to the left, and an air speed indicator, fuel gauge and watch to the right. A hand pump was provided to top up the air pressure in the tank if required and a blip switch was mounted on the top of the control column.

Two prototypes, 7456 and 7457, were commissioned, the first being completed and ready for inspection on 6 October 1915; however,

The second prototype F.E.8, 7457, at St Omer in December 1915. The gun is mounted in the centre of the nose and controlled by the sighting bar in front of the windscreen that moved in parallel with it.

it did not make its first flight by Frank Goodden until 15 October when if flew for just ten minutes. Its next flight on 19 October lasted an hour and a half with Goodden finding no fault of any kind. By 5 November, it had been painted with the standard service finish, PC10, and was at the Central Flying School for evaluation. The report stated:

Stability: excellent in all axes. Not at all tiring to fly.
Remarks: the hand pressure pump and 2-way tap might be removed to a more convenient location. Machine is very satisfactory and easy to fly. Being small and high powered, it naturally requires careful handling, especially of the rudder. The seating accommodation is comfortable but rather too much lying back. Pilot would be more comfortable sitting straighter. Machine gun, as now fitted, is rather low and difficult to reload. It is suggested that the gun mounting be raised at least six inches, the pistol grip then being in line with the top of the control column. The machine is in every other respect highly satisfactory, and very handy and controllable and extremely easy to land. Windscreen fitted is efficient and goggles can be dispensed with. Controllability on the ground is good.

The Central Flying School noted that the take-off run was 60 yards and the landing run 90 yards, both fairly typical figures for those days. Also, its top speed was 94 mph, a slightly lower figure than that recorded while under test flying at Farnborough. On 15 November, it was returned to Farnborough by the famous pre-war display pilot B. C. Hucks who had the misfortune to crash on landing, damaging 7456 beyond repair. By this time, the second prototype, 7457, was almost complete and using the engine recovered from 7456, made its first flight piloted by Goodden on 6 December recording a speed of 97.4 mph. It was initially, and for no apparent reason, fitted with a conical spinner to the propeller hub, but was otherwise identical to 7456. On 18 December 1915, Mervyn O'Gorman, Superintendent of the Royal Aircraft Factory, wrote the following note to Brig-Gen. Hugh Trenchard, Commander of the RFC in France:

I am sending you, piloted by Goodden, my F.E.8 fighter. I would like to draw to your notice some points both as regards stability and the fighting qualities of this machine. The machine is absolutely stable fore and aft, and laterally, and may be flown with all controls free. The directional stability is such that the machine will fly straight with the feet off the rudder bar.

On the following day, 7457 was flown to France by Goodden for service trials. It joined No. 5 Squadron that was operating the first DH2s alongside the Vickers FB5 and for whom the Gnome Monosoupape engine held few surprises. 7457 was flown by Lt Powell who took to it immediately stating that 'every detail of the F.E.8 was so far advanced from the DH2' although he, like the Central Flying School, was critical of the gun mounting. Nor did Powell like the propeller spinner that he claimed vibrated and was removed. Powell took 7457 on a patrol and in an engagement with an enemy two-seater, received bullet damage to his petrol tank, but managed to glide home. No spares were yet available and with repair of the tank causing some concern, 7457 was grounded until the undamaged tank from 7456 could be shipped over.

Trenchard, having discussed the machine's performance and handling with Powell, wanted the endurance increased from 2½ hours to 3 hours, but the necessary increase in petrol tank capacity proved impossible without a major redesign of the nacelle; however, an increase from 25 gallons to 29 gallons was achieved for all future machines giving an endurance of 2¾ hours. He also accepted the criticism of the gun installation and requested that the Royal Aircraft Factory send an engineer to France to arrange the necessary modifications as soon as possible. As a result, the gun was moved to the cockpit rim on a mounting similar to that of the DH2. The hole left in the nose by the removal of the gun was faired over and ammunition racks fitted to the nacelle side. Thus modified, 7457 remained with No. 5 Squadron, Powell choosing it in preference to the DH2 and refusing leave rather than risk another pilot flying it.

On 17 January 1917, Powell shot down an Aviatik and claimed a second kill on 5 February. On the same day, he chased an Albatros over the lines but failed to shoot it down, but was credited with an L.V.G. two-seater 'driven down'. A similar claim for an Albatros two days later was not confirmed, but on 29 February, he sent an Aviatik down in flames.

The first prototype, 7456, was rebuilt to production standard and was completed by early April. It remained at Farnborough and was tested with the 110-hp Le Rhône and Clerget engines, installations which necessitated modifications to the fuel-feed systems and engine controls in each case. The Gnome, however, remained the standard fitting. Production was undertaken by the Darracq Motor Engineering Co. Ltd and Vickers with the first completed example from Darracq joining No. 29 Squadron on 15 June 1916. This example was shot down a week later on 22 June and its pilot, Capt. L. Sweet, killed. At least five examples of the F.E.8—6378, 6380, 6381, 6383 and 6385—served with No. 29 Squadron alongside its DH2s.

Lt Fredrick Powell demonstrates the extent of movement possible with the modified gun mounting of a well-worn 7457. The hole in the nose has been covered by an aluminium disc and racks for ammunition drums have been added.

– F.E.8, 6390, showing the rubber bungees which returned the ailerons to their original position. The pilot's lap strap can be seen hanging over the side of the cockpit.

The introduction of the F.E.8 was greeted with a similar fear of spinning as that of the DH2 earlier in the year. However, the Royal Aircraft Factory took prompt action and on 23 August, the results of spin trials conducted in 7456 by Goodden were circulated. His report included what was probably the first ever published instruction on spin recovery:

1] - Switch off motor.
2] - Control stick put central and pushed forward.
3] - Rudder put in centre.

This results in a nosedive from which the aeroplane, having once got up to speed, can easily be pulled out with the control stick pulled back slightly.

The first squadron to be fully equipped with the F.E.8 was No. 40 under the command of Major Robert Loraine and with Frederick Powell as a flight commander. Powell thought Loraine as rather heavy handed, both as a pilot and superior officer, but welcomed the promotion and opportunity to continue flying the F.E.8. 'A' Flight went to France on 2 August 1916 and suffered its first casualty with the loss of Lt Davies in 7595 the following day. 'B' and 'C' Flights flew to France as soon as sufficient aeroplanes were available and the squadron based at Treizzennes was not complete until 25 August.

Their first victory came on 22 September when Capt. D. O. Mulholland in 6084 spotted a Fokker attacking an F.E.2b and went to its assistance, shooting down the enemy fighter (both Mulholland and the F.E.2b crew claimed credit for the kill). On the same day, 2 Lt Hay engaged a Roland two-seater, but the encounter was inconclusive. On 20 October, Mulholland shot down two Fokkers with Lt E. L. Benbow claiming an Albatros and S. A. Sharpe a Roland. The following day, Benbow sent a two-seater down in flames near Vimy. The squadron claimed a total of five enemy machines, a feat that was congratulated by Trenchard with a signal followed by a personal visit a few days later.

By this time, a second F.E.8 squadron was in action in France. No. 41 Squadron had arrived on 15 October with just twelve of eighteen aircraft that had taken off from Gosport for St Omer with mechanical problems and forced landings accounting for the other six. After a week to regroup, the squadron moved to Abeele where ground crews and equipment caught up with them. They began operations only to discover that their pushers were significantly outclassed by the latest

Two No. 40 Squadron F.E.8s outside the sheds at their base at Trezziennes. The large numerals on the nacelles indicate their flight numbers. (*David Gunby*)

Mechanics of No. 40 Squadron stand proudly with one of the squadron's F.E.8s soon after their arrival in France. (*David Gunby*)

F.E.8, 6410, with No. 40 Squadron at Trezziennes. (*David Gunby*)

No. 41 Squadron F.E.8, 7616, in flight. The streamers attached to the rear interplane struts indicate that it was leading a patrol.

German machines. The squadron's duties were largely ground attack and their first victory was achieved on 24 January 1917, the successful pilot, Cecil Tooms, being shot down just hours later.

On 9 November 1916, Capt. Tom Mapplebeck, a flight commander with No. 40 Squadron, was shot down during an engagement with Jasta 8 and his F.E.8, 7624, landed behind enemy lines and was captured more or less intact. It was test flown by the Germans for evaluation purposes with black crosses painted over its British markings.

Problems were experienced with the fuel feed, it proving difficult to maintain pressure when the tanks were nearly empty and 6426 was therefore fitted with the gravity tank from a DH2 in addition to its pressure tank. This solved the issue but its drag cut at least 4 mph from the machine's top speed. Therefore, an internal tank was made from sheet copper by Sgt Ridley to fit inside the centre section. This solved the fuel feed problems without a reduction in speed and so copies of this tank were manufactured in England and shipped out to be fitted to all F.E.8s in service.

It was discovered that after a time in the field, electrolytic corrosion was occurring between the duralumin ribs of the elevators and the steel tube frame to which they were fixed. 7456 was therefore fitted with the elevators of a DH2, the hinge positions being suitably modified. Other machines were similarly fitted until replacement elevators with wooden ribs could be manufactured.

No. 40 Squadron's Lt Benbow shot down a two-seater on 16 November and an Albatros DII fighter on 4 December with Mulholland scoring the same day. Benbow's success with the F.E.8 continued into 1917 and on 14 February, he downed an Albatros DII while flying A4871. Benbow also shot down another Albatros the same day. Lt John Hay of No. 40 Squadron scored three victories flying 6388, but fell victim to the guns of an Albatros DII flown by Manfred von Richthofen on 23 January 1917. This was the Red Baron's seventeenth victory and the first with Jasta II.

Capt. R. H. Saundby, who joined No. 41 Squadron at the end of January 1917, shared a victory on 4 March when flying 6431 in company with 2 Lt A. Fraser in 7622. He spotted a Nieuport in combat with an Albatros and immediately dived to assist in sending the enemy down.

The F.E.8's career with No. 40 Squadron effectively ended in March 1917 after nine machines took part in a lengthy dogfight with Albatros DIIs of Richthofen's Jasta II and all were shot down, five of them being destroyed. The squadron began to swap its F.E.8s for the new Nieuport 17 almost immediately, although a number of the squadron's pilots who

No. 40 Squadron's, 6456, was shot down on 9 March 1917 by Ltn Kurt Wolfe of Jasta II (his second victory).

German soldiers guard A4874 after it came down behind the lines on 9 March 1917.

had never flown anything but pushers found the reduction in a forward view a disadvantage.

No. 41 Squadron began the process of changing over to the DH5 on 11 June 1917, scoring a final victory with the F.E.8 on 16 June with the changeover completed by the beginning of July. But this was not the end of the F.E.8's role in the war. As like most outdated fighters, it carried on serving with training and home defence units in the UK. Lionel Blaxland, later a county cricketer, flew an F.E.8 with No. 61 (HD) Squadron at Rochford and wrote of it:

> The F.E.8 was a very pleasant machine to fly, but was extremely cold. I recall one of our pilots having to be helped out of his machine and, on putting his feet to the ground, having his legs give way under him.

One example, A4919, was handed over to a French liaison officer on 30 September 1917 in rather mysterious circumstances for no one knew why they wanted it. Having arrived in a crate at the Aircraft Acceptance Park at Hendon towards the end of the September, it was assembled and on 29 September, test flown by A. G. D. Alderson who recalled:

> I took my seat in the nacelle which felt very strange after a tractor, it being impossible to see any part of the machine from the cockpit.

Alderson commented more favourably on the unobstructed forward view.

The following day, A4919 was flown away and never heard of again—an appropriate end to a machine that, despite the excellence of its design, arrived too late to do any good and had long outlived its usefulness.

CHAPTER 3

Flawed Fighters

As the war progressed, there were attempts to think outside the box and design fighter aeroplanes that broke the established pattern and introduced a new idea. Some of the better innovative designs possessed sufficient merit to make it into production and service. However, a number lacked the vital spark of genius that made a useful fighter into a great one and the innovation that made them different proved to be a flaw.

VICKERS FB19

The FB19 was an attempt to correct the flaws of the earlier ES1 on which it was based, the design being taken over by George Challenger, Vickers' chief designer. Following the basic layout at its predecessor, a rather tubby looking biplane with a wingspan of just over 24 feet, Challenger's initial design had the cockpit located between the un-staggered wings, but introduced a large cut-out in the trailing edge of the upper wing to improve the pilot's view upwards. Short semi-conical fairings blended the curve of the engine cowling into the fuselage well ahead of the cockpit where the fuselage sides were flat, improving the pilot's view downwards. The fuselage remained un-tapered in elevation to a point aft of the cockpit, making it appear stubby and smaller than it was. Various other detail changes were made to improve the design although the neatly curved fin and rudder resembled that of the ES1. The Vickers gun was mounted in a recess on the portside of the fuselage in a lower position than on the ES1, again synchronised by the indigenous Vickers-Challenger gear and firing through a hole in the engine cowling, clear of the spinning cylinders.

Four examples were built at Vickers' Weybridge works, the first, A1968, fitted with a 100-hp Gnome Monosoupape engine and the remainder with the 110-hp Clerget. A1968 appears to have made its first flight before its gun was installed as did A1969 that differed (as

Close-up of the forward fuselage of an unidentified FB19 showing the installation of the Vickers gun, the operating rod of its synchronisation gear below it, and the hole in the cowling through which the bullets passed.

well as having the Clerget engine) in having a clear vision panel in the upper centre section to further improve the pilot's upward view which, although better than that of the ES1, remained poor. Its performance was meagre with a top speed of 98 mph, a fairly leisurely climb, and a ceiling of just under 17,000 feet—figures bettered by its contemporary rival, the iconic Sopwith Pup. The third machine, A2122, which also had a clear vision panel, was flown by Harold Barnwell to Farnborough for AID inspection on 18 July. It was allotted to the RFC in France the following day although this was cancelled two days later and the machine assigned to home defence duties where it was joined by the fourth and final machine built for the RFC, A2992, on 11 August.

In service, the type was known as the Vickers 'Bullet', a title inherited from its predecessor, the visually similar ES1.

A2992 went to No. 50 (HD) Squadron and was stationed at Dover. On 22 September 1916 and piloted by Maj. M. G. Christie, it took off with other machines in pursuit of an unidentified enemy aircraft that was attacking the town. Christie spotted the raider and chased it for some time until it disappeared into the clouds whereupon he returned to the aerodrome. This appears to have been as close as the FB19 ever got to the enemy.

A number (possibly as many as fifty) were fitted with the 110-hp Le Rhône 9J engine and delivered to Russia, presumably as a result of the Imperial Air Service's Commission visit to Vickers' Erith works the previous year when they were shown the ES1. Some were destroyed in their packing cases during the revolution, but a few were taken over by the Bolshevik Workers' and Peasants' Air Fleet and flown adorned with red star markings.

Following the type's failure to meet the approval of the RFC in the autumn of 1916, Challenger further modified the design by staggering the wings so as to improve the upward view from the cockpit. This necessitated modifying the fuselage frame so that the lower wing could be attached eleven inches further back while the upper wing was moved forwards a similar distance in order to keep the centre of pressure in the same location as previously. In other respects, the machine remained unaltered and was designated as the FB19 Mk II, although it was officially known as the Vickers Scout and more commonly as the Vickers 'Bullet'.

In mid-October, Vickers informed the War Office that if an order was placed immediately, delivery could be made by 20 November, otherwise it would be greatly delayed. Whether Vickers had another contract or this was pure salesmanship spin is unclear; however, an order for twelve machines was placed on 23 October without a prototype being produced. Clearly, the alterations to what was otherwise an existing design were easily achieved as the first Mk II, A5174, was flown out to No.1 depot at St Omer on 2 November. It was then moved to No. 2 depot at Candas on 10 November before flown to No. 20 Squadron at Fienvillers by Capt. W. Patrick. After initial evaluation flights, it was discovered that several ribs were broken in the lower port wing and an investigation revealed that Challenger had not made any provision for the additional stresses caused by staggering the wings. Fortunately, the remedy was simple—to introduce compression ribs of solid ash, which was done to A5174 at the depot, and to all uncompleted machines (A5225–5236) at the Factory.

On 1 December, A5174 moved on for assessment by pilots of No. 70 Squadron and on 11 December, it was returned to No. 2 depot. On 11 November, Brooke-Popham informed the Director of Aeronautical Equipment that owing to the current shortage of fast aeroplanes, the design would be useful as an interim measure. However, he later appears to have changed his mind as on 19 December, A5174 was returned to the UK in a crate.

No other FB19s went to France, the remainder of the batch being assigned to the less demanding theatre of war in the Middle East where there was an urgent demand for fighters. The FB19s arrived at 'X' depot in Egypt (the supply centre for the Eastern Mediterranean) during June 1917. At least one was with No. 47 Squadron in Macedonia by mid-July and several went to No. 14 Squadron in Palestine. When No. 111 Squadron was formed on 1 August and stationed at Deir-El-Belah in Gaza, it was equipped with the assorted fighter types then available. A5226 and A5227 formed part of its initial equipment, being joined by the remainder of the FB19s from No. 14 Squadron a week or so later and by the end of September, the squadron had five in service.

FB19 Mk II, A5234, in Palestine showing the staggered wings. The centre section has both a trailing edge cut-out and a clear vision panel, both intended to further improve the upward view.

A5225 with No. 47 Squadron personnel. The boy would appear to be ill at ease and may not have been a regular visitor.

Encounters with the enemy were few and mostly inconclusive, especially as the view from the cockpit remained poor and pilots complained of losing sight of their opponent in combat. Its top speed was 98 mph at 10,000 feet and it took nearly 15 minutes to reach that height. On 4 October, Lt C. R. Davidson, flying A5233 over Huj-Beit, claimed to have shot down an Albatros DIII and was awarded the victory. However, records show no corresponding loss by the enemy that day, the Albatros probably having feigned defeat in order to break off combat and escape, and so Davidson's victory was merely a moral one. Two other 'out of control' victories were claimed by pilots flying the FB19.

The end of October saw an increase in aerial activity in preparation for the third Battle of Gaza, but it brought no increase in the success rate for the FB19. In December 1917, Brig-Gen. W. S. Brancker, then commanding the RFC's Middle East Brigade, stated bluntly in a memo to his superior officer that 'Vickers "Bullets" are not very much good'. By the end of the year, they had almost been withdrawn from active

A mechanic poses as though about to swing the propeller of a No. 111 Squadron FB19 Mk II.

A5236 with No. 111 Squadron in the Middle East.

service, No. 111 Squadron exchanging the last of its FB19s for an S.E.5a in early January 1918. Thus released from frontline duties, a few of the tubby scouts found their way to the School of Aerial Fighting at Heliopolis with at least one being extant as late as 1919. Some may have been shipped back to the UK, several being reported at Joyce Green, an aerodrome adjoining the Vickers works at Erith in Kent, on home defence duties; however, as in other areas of operation, they achieved little of note.

A civil registration, G-EAAV, was allotted to a Vickers 'Bullet' in May 1919, but was cancelled in July the same year and appears not to have been taken up.

AIRCO DH5

Designed during 1916, the DH5 was the Aircraft Manufacturing Company's attempt to combine the aerodynamic efficiency of a tractor type with the forward view of a pusher. Its single bay wings of equal span were given a considerable negative stagger, the leading edge of the upper wing thus being located immediately above the pilot's head. The fuselage comprised of the usual four longerons and was built in two halves, joined aft of the cockpit, plywood stiffeners added to the wire cross bracing to increase its rigidity. The prototype had its 110-hp Le Rhône rotary engine enclosed in a plain open front cowling that was faired in to the flat sides of the fuselage, the tips of the semi-conical fairings extending to the cockpit. The high-aspect-ratio ailerons were not fitted with balance cables, but were held in their flying position by rubber bungees.

On completion of test flying, which was carried out both by de Havilland and B. C. Hucks, the DH5 was sent to France for evaluation, arriving at No. 1 depot at St Omer on 26 October. After a similar visit to No. 2 depot at Candas, it was flown to Farnborough by Flt Sgt M. Piercey on 18 November. A suggestion forwarded by Brig-Gen. Brooke-Popham to the Director of Aeronautical Equipment was that the centre section covering should be omitted to improve the reward view. This was accepted; however, the change was never implemented.

A5172, as the prototype DH5 had become, next went to the Central Flying School whose report dated 9 December 1916, largely ignored its most obvious feature and evaluated its performance as follows:

Stability: quite satisfactory. Lateral and longitudinal very good. Directional fair.

Controllability: quite satisfactory. Machine easy to land and to fly, handy and quick in the air.

Tactical Features: Vickers gun fired by pilot through the propeller and can be elevated about 60 degrees from the horizontal.

Facilities for reconnaissance good.

The view forward, upwards and downwards is very good. The view behind is badly masked by top plane.

Its top speed at 10,000 feet was measured as 102 mph, which although slightly inferior to the Sopwith Pup that was then just entering service, was a considerable improvement on the pusher types it was intended to replace. On 15 January 1917, the first contracts were placed for mass production. The Aircraft Manufacturing Company was to build a total of 200 (A9163–9361) including the prototype, A5172, and the Darracq Motor Engineering Co. was to build a similar number (A9363–9562). Further orders were later placed with the British Caudron Company for fifty machines and in March, Jones and Cribb Ltd of Leeds were contracted for 100, although deliveries from this company were very slow and it is possible that the contract was not fulfilled. Production machines differed from the prototype in having a revised fuel system, incorporating a gravity tank mounted on the starboard wing root, and had their fuselages faired to a circular cross section. Balance cables for the ailerons were introduced during production, although examples built with rubber bungees retained them until written off.

The prototype DH5 at Hendon showing the semi-conical fairings which blended the circular engine cowling into the flat-sided fuselage and the rubber bungees holding the ailerons in flying position.

A side view of the prototype DH5 at Hendon showing the extent of the negative stagger to the wings.

A9288 shows the fully-faired fuselage of production DH5s and the slipstream-driven fuel pump mounted on the starboard undercarriage leg.

Structural tests, which were carried out during April before the type entered service, revealed that the wings could withstand almost seven-and-a-half times their normal load without failure, well in excess of the desired factor of safety of six (the flying wire attachment bolt being the first component to fail). Nos 24 and 32 Squadrons changed from the DH2 to the DH5 during May 1917, the first production machine from Airco being with No. 24 Squadron by 1 May while the first example from Darracq was delivered to Farnborough on 9 May. No. 41 Squadron also converted to the DH5, finally giving up its F.E.8s, and was operational with its new mounts by the end of July.

Although an improvement over the pushers it had replaced, the DH5's single Vickers gun made it inferior to the S.E.5 that came into use at the same time as well as the Sopwith Camel (that arrived in France in July), both of which had two machine guns. It was also inferior to the latest German fighters, many of which had been fitted with two guns since the previous autumn. Initially, the Constantinesco gear, which synchronised the gun's firing to miss the propeller blades, proved troublesome until mid-June when the necessary modification to the trigger motor was made available. Nonetheless, No. 24 Squadron was able to achieve its first confirmed victory with the type on 25 May when 2 Lt S. Cockerell in A9363 sent down an Albatros DIII that was seen to crash. Lt W. H. Stratham accounted for another Albatros three days later and yet during its whole time in action, the squadron would claim just two more enemy aircraft destroyed while flying the DH5. In the words of the squadron's historian: 'Unfortunately, the new machine was a failure.' However, Capt. J. E. Doyle, who contributed extensively to aviation magazines between the wars, recalled 'I found it a most comfortable and pleasant machine to fly, extremely sensitive to aileron control.' Lt A. King Cowper, an Australian pilot who joined No. 24 Squadron in the autumn of 1917 and shot down two Albatros DIIs while flying the DH5, said of it:

> I found this machine very manoeuvrable and thus a very good fighting aircraft. But having a backward wing stagger, it was completely blind for rear vision, therefore a dangerous aircraft. For ground observation, it was ideal, having such a marvellous forward vision.

Its forward vision made it ideal for ground attack, a role into which it was first put during the Third Battle of Ypres that began in June 1917 and continued bogged down in the Flanders mud at Passchendaele until November. Often fitted with racks to carry four 25-lb cooper bombs to augment its single machine gun, the role led to high losses, although those for the DH5 were no worse than for any other type carrying out similar operations.

The enemy were presented with an example for evaluation in early September when No. 24 Squadron's A9435 was forced to land behind the lines and captured intact, its pilot, 2 Lt G. P. Robertson, taken prisoner. On 29 October, No. 41 Squadron's A9474 suffered a similar fate as it was also forced down behind the lines and captured intact. Regardless of what the enemy may have thought of it, the DH5 was not popular with its pilots. Also, in addition to other shortcomings, its landing speed was rather high for the time and vibration from the Le Rhône rotary engine made instruments difficult to read (although the engine bearer plate was later modified to reduce this problem). At least one example was fitted with a Clerget engine of similar power, but no improvement was found and the Le Rhône remained the standard fitting.

No. 68 Squadron, the second squadron formed with Australian personnel, left Harlaxon in Lincolnshire on 21 September 1917, arriving at its new base at Warloy, near Baizieux. The following day, it was equipped with fourteen DH5s, seven built by Airco, six by Darracq and one, B377, by The British Caudron Company. Additional machines arrived to bring the squadron up to strength within a week, but two accidents occurred on 1 October with A9242 written off when magneto

Australians of No. 68 Squadron pose with A9245 at Harlaxton before departing for France. A presentation machine, its inscription reads 'New South Wales N.16. The Upper Hunter Battleplane.' (*Australian War Memorial*)

failure necessitated a forced landing. Also, A9524 forced landed due to a mechanical failure but was later repaired. Both pilots, Lts D. Morrison and F. Huxley, were unhurt.

The next day, a patrol of four machines, led by Capt. W. McCloughty, dived down to attack a two-seater, which being faster than the DH5, escaped undamaged with several similar incidents occurring over the next few weeks. On 13 October, Lt Morrison engaged an Albatros, but was shot down and landed in no man's land. Although recovered by soldiers from the British trenches, Morrison died of his wounds and his machine, A9277, was shelled to destruction. The same day, the squadron practised bombing, the DH5s having been fitted with racks and release gear by mechanics, and their role changed to ground attack for the forthcoming Battle of Cambrai. Nonetheless, some combat patrols were flown with Lt Huxley scoring the squadron's first victory on 22 November when, piloting A9461, he shot down an Albatros. Capt. R. C. Phillips, while flying A9288, scored his first victory the same day. Lt G. Taylor claimed a DFW on 26 November with a few more being achieved before the squadron converted to the S.E.5a, returning its last DH5 to the depot on 19 December.

No. 64 Squadron, previously a training squadron, began converting to the DH5 at the beginning of July 1917. Unfortunately, it suffered an early casualty when A9393 broke up, shedding a wing as Capt. E. G.

The gravity tank on the upper-centre section can be clearly seen on A9513.

A9344 served with the Australians of No. 68 Squadron (2 Squadron AFC).

A9507 that served with No. 64 Squadron. Like many DH5s, it is a presentation machine given by the 'Christchurch Old Boys' Club'. The flight marking 'E' has had small letters added to form the name 'Elsa'. (*Colin Huston*)

Hanlon performed a loop on 26 July. The squadron left Sedgewick in the morning of 14 October, flying in formation to Lympne and St Omer in the afternoon. As the pilots were highly experienced, the move was made without loss and the next day, the squadron took up residence at Izel-le- Hameau. Flying ground attack missions on 20 November (the opening of the Battle of Cambrai), the squadron did good work, destroying a number of gun emplacements, but suffered the casualties typical of such efforts with Lt R. Angus shot down and killed in A9335, Lt L. Williams in A9406 wounded by ground fire and Lts O. Meredith and J. P. MaCrae unaccounted for (the latter was found to be a prisoner). At least two other machines, A9492 and A9235, were damaged, the former sufficiently to be returned to No. 2 depot at Candas, but their pilots were unhurt. As for other DH5 squadrons, combat victories were few with Capt. Slater scoring first on 30 November by sending a DFW two-seater down out of control and Capt. Tempest claiming an Albatros DV.

Although the arrival of No. 64 Squadron during October had brought the number of units operating the DH5 in France up to five, within weeks the process of converting to more effective aeroplanes began with No. 41 Squadron acquiring its first S.E.5a before the end of the month, completing the changeover during November. By the beginning of 1918, all DH5 squadrons had converted to the S.E.5a, No. 32 Squadron returning A9513, the last DH5 in active service, to the depot on 8 March. Inevitably, the type continued in use at training units, proving no more popular there than it had in France.

BRISTOL M1 MONOPLANE

By the beginning of 1916, designers knew what qualities a fighter aeroplane needed to possess: speed, manoeuvrability and a clear view. At the British and Colonial Aeroplane Company in Bristol, Frank Barnwell decided that a clean design could provide the speed. The compact mass of a rotary engine was needed to aid manoeuvrability and that the view above and behind would be enhanced by making the new design a monoplane: the M1. This was a brave decision as following a number of fatal accidents caused by structural failures the War Office had banned the use of monoplanes in September 1912 pending investigation. Although their use, subject to certain modifications was resumed the following spring, some prejudice undoubtedly remained.

The M1's fuselage was built around a conventional box frame of four longerons, but fully faired with formers and stringers to maintain a circular cross section as far back as the cockpit, then tapering

The original Bristol monoplane, the M1A, showing the half-hoop cabane struts over the cockpit.

to the rudder post. The 110-hp Clerget 9Z engine was enclosed in a circular cowling and fitted with the broad propeller spinner previously tested on Bristol 'Scout' 5555, a narrow gap between the spinner and cowling admitted air to the engine. The wings were attached to the upper longerons with flying wires running at a fairly shallow angle to the lower longerons. Landing wires were supported from a cabane structure comprising two flattened half hoops of streamlined steel tube immediately above the cockpit. Three tanks held a total of 17½ gallons of petrol limiting the type's endurance to less than two hours.

The prototype (work number 1374) made its first flight at Filton piloted by Fred Raynham on 14 July 1916 and recorded a maximum speed of 132 mph, significantly faster than any machine then available. When tested at the Central Flying School, its speed at low level was not measured as the propeller was intended to enhance performance at altitude—128 mph at 5,000 feet was recorded and its climb to 10,000 feet took just 8½ minutes. The CFS report, No. M21, was scarcely enthusiastic and stated bluntly:

> Stability: lateral very good, longitudinal fairly good, directional good.
> Length of run to unstuck 85 yards, to pull up (engine stopped) 114 yards.
> Control: machine tiring to fly. Requires good pilot. Moderate ease of landing. Machine is nose heavy when gliding. Tendency to turn right with engine on.

However, on 9 October, the War Office issued contract 87/A/61 purchasing the prototype to which the serial A5138 was assigned and ordering a further four examples, A5139–5142. These differed from the original in having a simplified cabane structure comprising four straight steel tubes arranged in a pyramid and were designated type M1B. They were fitted with a Vickers gun, mounted over the upper longeron on the portside, and had a cut-out between the spars on the starboard wing root to provide an improved downward view. Two examples were fitted with 110-hp Le Rhône engines, the third having a Clerget of 130 hp, and the fourth an early example of the new AR1 rotary developed by W. O. Bentley rated at 150 hp. Remarkably, the performance of the two machines fitted with higher-rated engines proved inferior to the original when tested at the Central Flying School. The stall speed was recorded as 52 mph giving a fairly high landing speed and apparently led to a decision that the type would not be suitable for use on the small landing fields in France. This decision probably reflected some residual

M1B, A5139, showing how the Vickers gun was offset to port and mounted above the longeron. Seen here at Hounslow, it was at No. 2 depot in Candas on 14 February 1917.

prejudice against monoplanes as other types, such as the DH2 already in service, had landing speeds almost as high and many required far longer landing runs and yet operated in France without undue issues.

Three machines, A5140, A5141 and A5142, were shipped to the Middle East, arriving at the depot in Egypt in June 1917. They served first with No. 14 Squadron and one crashed on 3 August after suffering engine failure on take-off. They were then transferred to No. 111, joining 'A' Flight a week after its formation on 1 August, and proved popular with pilots although their limited endurance rendered them unsuitable for escorting reconnaissance machines across the long distances involved in the desert war and severely limited their operational usefulness. However, on 29 October, Lt A. H. Peck in A5142 engaged a Rumpler but was unable to bring it down. A5141 landed in territory held by the Turks on 25 November after running out of fuel. Its pilot, Edgar Percival (who later founded the aircraft company that bore his name) made it back to his base and the aircraft was later recovered and reassigned to a training unit. A5140 was struck off charge on 1 December and the following day, A5142 crashed and was returned to the depot for repair. Its last recorded operational flight was made when it took off to pursue an enemy aircraft that flew over the aerodrome but failed to intercept it.

Two M1Bs with No. 111 Squadron in the Middle East. Nearest the camera is A5141.

Like the Vickers FB19, Brig-Gen. W. S. Brancker, then commanding the RFC in the Middle East, considered that the M1Bs were 'Not very much good.' However, this opinion stated in December 1917 after their use had ceased was already too late as on 3 August a contract had been placed for 125 to be built. Given the serials C4901-C5025, they were powered by the 110-hp Le Rhône engine, had their Vickers guns mounted on the fuselage centreline in the pilot's line of sight and synchronised by the hydraulic CC (George Constantinescu) gear, cuts outs provided in both wing roots and were designated as the M1C.

Production preceded quickly, the first example being delivered on 19 September. Six machines were shipped to Chile in part payment for two warships, *Almirante Lattore* and *Almirante Cochrane*, which were built in British shipyards and taken over by the Royal Navy on completion. One of these machines was flown by Lt Dagoberto Godoy from Santiago to Mendoza in Argentina and back again making what was claimed to be the first aerial crossing of the Andes in the process. Godoy took the precaution of wrapping his body in newspaper as extra protection against the cold at high altitudes before making the flight.

By the end of the 1917, fifteen examples had been dispatched to the depot in Egypt, a further eighteen following in the New Year. Fewer than twenty saw active service, some of the remainder remaining in Egypt for use in training at Heliopolis.

No. 72 Squadron (which after forming up in England and regrouped at Basrah in what was then Mesopotamia on 2 March) included eight Bristol M1Cs in its mixed collection of aircraft. A spirited display of aerobatics by two of the squadron's M1Cs was instrumental in persuading the Kurds to swear allegiance to the British cause. The squadron, in addition to reconnaissance and army co-operation, flew

Publicity photograph of M1C, C4910. The trestle holding the tail into flying position has been crudely deleted.

C4902, the second production M1C. It crashed on 19 October 1917.

A line up of M1Cs with No. 72 Squadron. The removal of the spinner spoiled both the appearance and streamlining, but assisted engine cooling in the desert heat.

ground-attack missions and assisted in the capture of Kifri and Kirkuk to the north of the region. It was common practice for the spinners to be removed in service in the desert. This ultimately changed their appearance and spoiled the streamlining, but greatly improving engine cooling.

Nos 17 and 47 Squadrons, both operating in Macedonia, each had a few M1Cs on strength, some of which they passed on to No. 150 Squadron when it was formed as a fighter unit on 1 April 1918.

Lt A. E. de M. Jarvis, a Canadian pilot, scored one of the M1C's few victories on 25 April when he shot down a DFW and shared another kill with an S.E.5a during the same mission. The next day, he, together with some others, attacked an enemy two-seater and shot it down.

On 16 June, Lt J. Harvey of No. 150 Squadron, attacked a Rumpler and believed he had shot it down, but was unable to observe it as he was attacked by an Albatros DIII, although he managed to break away. Another pilot from No. 150 Squadron, Lt K. B. Moseley, shot down an Albatros DV on 9 July and then claimed a DFW on 26 July. Capt. F. D. Travers, also from No. 150 Squadron, claimed a total of five enemy

The ace James McCudden with an unidentified M1C while serving as an instructor at a School of Aerial Fighting.

The last production M1C, C5025, in what was almost certainly the most elaborate markings applied to the type at the No. 3 School of Aerial Fighting, Bircham Newton.

aircraft shot down during the first two weeks of September while flying C4976, after which he changed to operating an S.E.5a and scored further victories.

Losses included an M1C shot down over Lake Doijan on 3 September. By the end of the month, the M1C had been withdrawn from service in the region, being replaced by more favoured aeroplanes such as the S.E.5a and Sopwith Camel. A number of M1Cs that remained in the UK were assigned to training units, especially to the Schools of Aerial Fighting based at Turnberry, Montrose, Hounslow and Marske-by-the-Sea where they were often adopted as personal mounts by instructors and occasionally painted in colourful schemes.

After the armistice in 1918, four examples were returned to the Bristol Company, one being sold to Spain with a second going to the USA. Another joined the civil register as G-EASR and the fourth, registered G-EAVP, was employed in trials of the Bristol Lucifer 100-hp three-cylinder radial engine and designated as the M1D. Piloted by Cyril Unwins, it won the 1923 Aerial Derby and was fitted with an engine uprated to 140 hp to compete for the Grosvenor Cup, but crashed at Chertsey while on route to Croydon, killing its pilot, Leslie Foot.

Henry John (Harry) Butler, who served as an instructor at the School of Aerial Fighting at Marske-by-the-Sea, bought two aeroplanes, an Avro 504 and an M1C, when he left the RAF in 1919. Both were shipped to his native Australia with a view to starting various aerial enterprises, including passenger flights and airmail delivery. He used the

Bristol to win the first Australian Aerial Derby on 8 September 1920. Butler died in 1924 as a result of complications arising from a crash in the Avro. The Bristol, formerly C5001 and then VH-UQI, passed into new ownership. It was later fitted with an inline engine and the fairings were removed from the fuselage leaving it slab sided. Painted bright red, it remained in use up to the outbreak of the Second World War and was the last Bristol monoplane in existence.

MARTINSYDE F4 'BUZZARD'

The F1 was a two-seater, based on an enlarged version of Martinsyde's G100 'Elephant', and powered by the newly introduced 250-hp Rolls-Royce Falcon engine, the F2 being a similar machine fitted with a 200-hp Hispano-Suiza. Neither was adopted for production and during the summer of 1917, George Handasyde developed the design into a single-seat fighter to be powered by a new version of the Rolls-Royce Falcon V12 water-cooled engine uprated to 285 hp.

Although of conventional appearance (its fuselage was built around the usual box girder), its unusual features included longerons of hickory and cross bracing to the forward portion by diagonal struts rather than wires. The upper decking was very deep and housed the fuel tanks and twin Vickers guns ahead of the cockpit, forming a head rest behind. The upper wing had a slightly greater span than the lower, both being of equal chord, braced in a single bay and with their leading edges covered with plywood to a point just aft of the main spar that was built of laminated spruce. Ailerons were fitted to all four wings and the vertical tail surfaces had the usual and rather elegant shape typical of Martinsydes—the tailplane incidence being adjustable by means of a trim wheel close to the pilot's left hand. Flight instrumentation was typical for the period with an air speed indicator, altimeter, clinometer and compass. Engine management consisted of a tachometer, fuel and oil pressure gauges, and ignition switches mounted on the instrument panel. Throttle, mixture adjustment and spark control were located to the pilot's left, and the petrol taps, hand pump (for fuel feed pressure) and radiator shutter control to his right. Also, provision was made for the stowage of oxygen cylinders in the lower fuselage. Throughout with its thorough cockpit and construction design, the Martinsyde's attention to detail was superb.

Its potential was spotted by engineers of the American Bolling Mission that toured Europe in June and July 1917 to select machines to be mass produced in America. The F3 was included in their list to be powered by the Liberty engine; however, the production programme stalled and no F3s were built.

The prototype, built without an official order, made its debut at Brooklands in September 1917 before going to Martlesham Heath for testing on 9 November where its performance was described in Report M158 as 'a great advance on all existing fighter scouts' with a top speed of 138 mph at 10,000 feet.

Six examples, B1490-1495, were built to contract AS.29238/17 for use in development of the design with one, B1490, fitted with a standard production Rolls-Royce Falcon engine, the lower output reducing the speed achieved at 10,000 feet to 130 mph (much faster than any rival design). Four of the initial batch appear not to have been required for testing or development and were assigned to home defence units. Two were issued to No. 39 Squadron based at North Weald to at least June 1918 and another, B1492, served at Biggin Hill with No. 141 Squadron.

With a performance superior to that of any contemporary design, it was decided that at least two squadrons should be equipped with the F3 and a production order was placed with Martinsyde for 150 machines (D4211-4360). However, as manufacture of the F3 got underway, it was realised that production of the Rolls-Royce Falcon could not keep pace with demand, principally for the two-seat Bristol F2b. Few, if any, would be available to power the Martinsyde leaving the company unable to fulfil the order and engineless airframes began to pile up at the Weybridge works.

Although ordered as an F3 with a Rolls-Royce engine, D4263, like most of the batch, was completed as an F4 and powered by a Hispano-Suiza.

D4353, although amongst the last of the batch of 150, appears to have been completed as an F3 with a V12 Rolls-Royce engine and fitted with a four-blade propeller.

Another view of D4353 showing the four-blade propeller to advantage.

In January 1918, George Handasyde modified his design to accommodate the 300-hp Hispano-Suiza V8 engine then being developed and made some changes to the lower wings to improve the downward view. The first engine was not delivered to Martinsyde's works until March when it was fitted to D4256 that was then tested at Martlesham Heath during June. Report M210 confirmed that its performance has surpassed the original with a top speed at sea level of 145 mph, making it one of the fastest aeroplanes then in existence.

Handasyde continued his development of the design, adopting D4214 for the purpose, moving the cockpit further aft, thereby adjusting the balance and improving the pilot's view as he was now clear of the upper wing. The ply covering to the forward fuselage was also extended further aft to suit the new cockpit location and the upper decking was similarly modified. The remainder of the batch were completed to the revised design and designated as the F4. At least one example was test flown at Martlesham Heath and possibly fitted with an alternative propeller, and higher speeds were recorded. The type was judged to be stable in flight, yet manoeuvrable and comfortable to fly, and it was decided that the F4 'Buzzard' would be a standard frontline fighter for 1919. A further contract for another 300 machines was therefore placed with Martinsyde and production orders also given to Boulton & Paul Ltd (500), Hooper & Co. (200) and the Standard Motor Company (300).

Although a long-range version, the 'Buzzard' Mk 1a was designed as an escort fighter for bombers of the Independent Force that planned to carry out strategic bombing raids into Germany; however, three prototypes were built and tested (H654–6542) yet no production orders were placed for it.

It was hoped that deliveries from the original batch of 150 would begin in August and be completed by November. However, deliveries of the Hispano-Suiza engines proved very slow and by the armistice on 11 November 1918, just fifty-seven examples of the earlier F3 model had been handed over to the RAF and none reached frontline service. Martinsyde were then instructed to only complete the machines they had started and orders placed with other manufacturers were cancelled. Despite the 'Buzzard's impressive performance, the post-war RAF would be equipped with the slower but cheaper Sopwith Snipe that was already in service.

One example was sent to France where, after comprehensive testing and evaluation, the type was selected to equip fighter units of the Aéronautique Militaire during 1919, but the war ended before they could be delivered. The USA also adopted the 'Buzzard' for its squadrons

D4256, the first to be fitted with the Hispano-Suiza engine showing the F4's very neat appearance. The aircraft behind its port wing is a Royal Aircraft Factory F.E.2b.

H6540 was the first of three 'Buzzards' modified to increase their endurance for long-range bombing missions.

H6542, one of three long-range 'Buzzard' Mk 1as at Kenley during 1919.

and planned to build 1,500 examples fitted with the 300-hp Hispano-Suiza to be built stateside; however, the war came to a close without any being completed.

During the post-war years, testing continued with both D4263 and D4264 delivered to Farnborough in early 1919 while D4269 was tested with an American-built engine. Two examples served with the RAF Communication Wing, shuttling back and forth between London and Paris during the 1919 Peace Conference, and on one occasion given a favourable wind, one covered the 215-mile journey in just 75 minutes. The type saw some service at the Central Flying School and one appeared in the RAF Pageant at Hendon in 1920.

Martinsyde Ltd eventually completed well over 300 examples, retaining some for private sales, and the type served in small numbers as both single and two-seaters with Ireland, Portugal, Finland, Spain and the Soviet Union. One example was shipped to Japan with the trade mission in 1921 and although no orders were forthcoming, the 'Buzzard' clearly influenced the design of Japanese aircraft for some time after. Civil-owned 'Buzzards' were employed as touring aircraft, racers—for which purpose alternative engines were occasionally fitted—and seal

Crowds examine a Martinsyde 'Buzzard' with what appears to be a race number on its rudder after the war. The aircraft in the background are a DH9 and DH4.

spotting in Canada.

Following the liquidation of Martinsyde in 1924, the remaining 'Buzzards' were acquired by the Aircraft Disposal Company of Croydon who continued to sell the aircraft to private customers as fast tourers and to foreign air services, eight examples going to Latvia fitted with Jaguar air-cooled radial engines. Six examples in Spain were still in service at the outbreak of the civil war in 1936. Those in service in Latvia lasted two years longer, testimony to the qualities of a design that was simply born too late for its intended role.

CHAPTER 4

The Forgotten Fighters Today

Few original examples of any of these aeroplanes survive today although reproductions of many of them can be found in museums around the world and kept, for exhibition flying, by enthusiasts.

The original machines include a Sopwith *Baby* at the Royal Navy's Fleet Air Arm Museum at Yeovilton in Somerset which, although displayed in the markings of N2078, was assembled, during the late 1960s, from parts of two machines which were sent to Italy during the war and later placed storage. Some missing parts had to be fabricated from scratch, and the propeller was located in Cyprus, were it was being displayed with a clock mounted in the centre. Although a hybrid it is about 90% original.

The Bristol M1C, VH-UQI which was originally shipped to Australia by Harry Butler has been re-fitted with a rotary engine and the fuselage fairings restored and, still painted bright red, is on public display in a small museum at Minlaton, South Australia, where Butler was based.

An original Martinsyde F4 *"Buzzard"* is on show, mounted on skis, in the Aviation Museum of Central Finland at Tikkakoshi, Jyvaskyla along with numerous other aeroplanes which served with the Finnish Air Force.

No examples of any of the other types have survived, although reproductions include a very accurate Sopwith Tabloid, G-BFDE built by Don Cashmore over a four year period in the late 1970's, in 1982, won the Popular Flying Associations' coveted "Best Replica" award, before being put on display at the RAF Museum at Hendon.

A non-flying reproduction Tabloid is currently under construction at Kingston University and, when completed, will be put on display locally to commemorate 100 years of aeroplane construction in Kingston-upon-Thames.

Another reproduction, built for sport flying, was completed in the USA during 2012, although its construction varies considerably from

The Sopwith *Baby* "N2078" on display in the entrance to the Fleet Air Arm Museum at Yeolvilton photographed around 1980. The logos on the floats and the fin are those of the Blackburn Aeroplane Company.

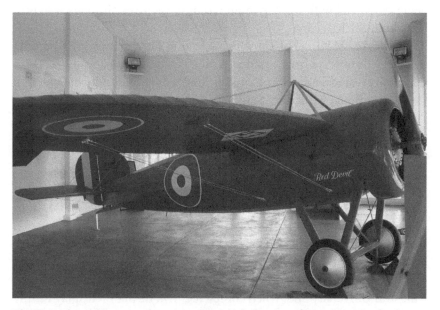

The Bristol M1C, restored to its original civilian configuration, on display at Minlaton, South Australia. (*Scott Butler*)

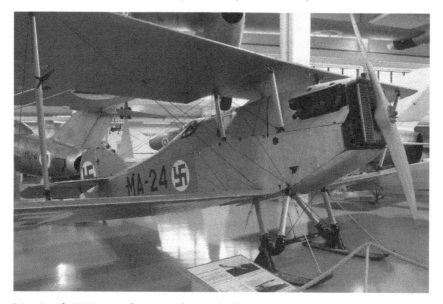

Martinsyde F4 *Buzzard* preserved in Finland.

Reproduction Sopwith *Tabloid* at the Popular Flying Association rally at Sywell in 1982 where it won the "Best replica" award.

that of the original and it is powered by a modified air-cooled 2.4 litre Volkswagen car engine concealed within the bull nosed cowling.

A reproduction Bristol Scout, N5419, was built, in the USA, by Leonard E. Opdycke, closely following the original plans, and made just one flight, in 1986, which was brought to an abrupt end by engine failure. Mr Opdycke, then publisher of the magazine *"WW1 Aero"* wrote the following account of that flight;-

"The machine lifted off easily and smoothly, and climb was also smooth. It flew hands off and was extremely manoeuvrable within the limits of what I chose to do. The only curiosity was that, in a steep turn, with the stick brought back to centre, the bank continued to increase until the stick was brought further back the other way.

After some 25 minutes of experimenting the magneto failed and the glide proved that the aircraft was as manoeuvrable and stable without power as with. The glide was satisfactory and the aeroplane was as stable as early pilots reported it, a delight to fly."

Repaired after the subsequent forced landing, it is now in the Fleet Air Arm Museum at Yeovilton where it is displayed stripped of its fabric covering so that its construction can be seen.

A static reproduction Scout D, built in 1962 by apprentices at the RAF's No.8 School of Technical Training is, at the time of writing, on display with the Shuttleworth Collection of Historic Aeroplanes at Old Warden Aerodrome in Bedfordshire, marked as A1742. Although not entirely accurate it gives a very good idea of how an original machine would have looked.

During the early 1960 a group of enthusiasts, based around Weybridge in Surrey, constructed a flying reproduction of a Vickers FB5. Given the civil registration G-ATVP, but marked as "2345"it appeared at a number of flying displays and is now on display at the Royal Air Force Museum at Hendon. At least one other reproduction example is believed to be in existence, marked as "A1452", its construction is more robust than that of original machines as it was originally built for film work and although unable to fly it has been taxied under its own power. Its current location is believed to be Sywell aerodrome in Northamptonshire, where it is displayed in the aerodrome museum.

Perhaps because of the novelty of its pusher configuration the DH2 has proved fairly popular with homebuilders in the USA where, in addition to several full size examples, a number of reduced scale reproductions have been built, often powered by inline engines concealed within the rear of the nacelle. One full scale example, G-BFVH, which is powered by a five cylinder radial engine, can also be seen in England. Originally built in 1978 by Vivian Bellamy, at his base near Lands End, it has

The Reproduction Bristol *Scout* built and flown by Leo Opdycke over the trees near Old Rhinebeck Aerodrome in New York State. (*via L.E. Opdycke*)

The Royal Air Force Museum's reproduction Vickers FB5 in flight soon after it was first built.

Flying reproduction DH2 based at Wickenby in Lincolnshire. Its radial engine has changed its flying characteristic, as well as its appearance, slightly form those of the original.

appeared in films and, after several changes of ownership, now resides at Wickenby, in Lincolnshire, from where it participates in occasional flying displays, marked as "5964", the machine in which Major L.G. Hawker was brought down.

Two reproduction F.E.8s are known to exist, both in the USA. The first was built by the late Cole Palen and his team back in the 1970s from original drawings which its construction, Palen told the author, " *he followed pretty closely, although not to every nut and bolt size*". Powered by an original rotary engine, it proved relatively easy to fly, at least to pilots accustomed to handling vintage aeroplanes, and performed regularly in the weekly air shows at Old Rhinebeck Aerodrome, in upper New York State. Palen bequeathed it to the National Air and Space Museum at the Smithsonian Institute in Washington D.C, where it still resides.

Another full scale reproduction is displayed at the Owls Head Transportation Museum in Maine, New England and powered by a modern 145 hp "*Continental*" air-cooled, flat six, engine, housed in the rear of the nacelle, which has been re-designed to accommodate it. Originally built in California by Jack Gardiner, in 1980 it made an epic cross-country trip to Maine, covering over 4,000 miles in 57 hours flying, spread over 32 days, on conclusion of which it was donated, by

Reproduction DH5 airborne over New Zealand, where it currently resides.

The Shuttleworth Collection's Bristol Monoplane flies regularly in displays of historic aeroplanes at its base in Bedfordshire

Gardiner, to the museum. Its civil registration, N928, is painted on the rudder so that it resembles an RFC serial number.

A full scale, flying reproduction DH5 was built in the USA by John Shively during the 1980s and registered as N950JS but marked with the serial A9507. Powered by a modern air cooled engine concealed within the cowling, and with modern flight instruments, it appeared in air shows in the UK in the early 1990s before returning to the USA and joining the late Frank Ryder's collection at Guntersville, Alabama. It is currently with the Vintage Aviator Collection at Hood aerodrome, Masterton, New Zealand and painted in the markings of A9242, a presentation aircraft which flew with 68 squadron RFC.

During the 1980's Northern Aeroplane Workshops, a group of talented enthusiasts based in Yorkshire, built a reproduction Bristol M1C monoplane following the original plans. Drawings for some metal components were only available in their completed state and had to be re-drawn as flat pieces of metals, ready for cutting out. The wings having an elegantly curved shape each of the clips which secure the leading edge to the ribs is different and the author was privileged to prepare the drawings for these, as well as for some other components. Powered, like the originals, by a 110hp *Le Rhone* rotary engine, the completed machine, G-BWJM, now forms part of the Shuttleworth Collection of Historic Aeroplanes and takes part in regular flying displays.

Another, equally accurate reproduction is on display at the Royal Air Force Museum at Hendon, in North London. Built by Don Cashmore and registered G-BLWM, it is currently marked as C4994.

Plans to build other reproductions are under consideration around the world but are, as yet, not sufficiently advanced for inclusion in this record.

Acknowledgements

In researching the material upon which this book is based I have received assistance, either with information or photographs, from many people to each of whom due acknowledgement, and my gratitude, is hereby be given. These include;- the late Jack Bruce, Ian Burns, Mick Davis, Peter Dye, Nick Forder, Peter Green, David Gunby, Colin and Barbara Huston, Phillip Jarrett, Kevin Kelly, Andy Kemp, Brian Kervell, Lanayre Liggera, Joan Loraine, Paul Leaman, Stuart Leslie, Leo Opdycke, the late Cole Palen, Peter Pountney, and numerous members of Cross & Cockade International, and WW1 aeroplanes Inc.

Any omissions from this list are due to oversight, not ingratitude, and should any mistakes have occurred, they remain, of course, my own.

A special and most heart felt thank you is long overdue to my wife, Linda, for putting up with living in a house filled with my research notes and papers, and for having to spend countless hours just watching me tapping on a computer keyboard.

Paul R. Hare
May 2014